"This book is published with the full permission and encouragement of Fluor Corporation. However, the opinions expressed in this book are those of the author and not of Fluor Corporation."

Praise for *Principle to Practice* and David Lynn

"David's effectiveness in interpreting OSHA's VPP practices encourages collaborative behavior in all aspects of work beyond safety. This simplification of the VPP process sustains the safety improvement culture and delivers long term organizational safety improvements."
—Chris H Evans MOHS, Executive HSE Director, Fluor Corporation.

"I worked for David while I was employed at OSHA, and I know he lives by the values and principles captured in his book. The most important lesson I learned from David was not how to interpret the regulations, but rather, how to implement them with passion and purpose. This book gives you a path to build an injury free culture and it also provides motivation to accomplish your goals. I even have a green ear for safety, if you read the book you'll understand!"
—Don Snizaski, President, Life & Safety Consultants, Inc.

"David's sports analogies drive home a key point. Winning teams start in the front office with management commitment. In the safety world, winning teams must have that same management commitment and a plan. Implementation of the 5 principles on a consistent basis will lay the ground work to achieve zero incidents. Winning with your safety plan and reaching zero incidents, will take an entire team commitment and effort. Challenge your team; Put VPP Principles to Practice should be the start of your game plan."
—Ric Carter, President, Fluor Constructors International, Inc.

"David's diverse background in the safety profession along with a straight forward approach provides any reader guaranteed success with implementing a complete Safety Program."
—John Spray, Senior Director, Operations & Maintenance, Fluor Global Services

"Lynn has a unique style of using personal real life experiences to get his safety message across. I recommend this book to anyone who has a personal passion for safety".
— David Webber, Corporate HSE, Director, US Operations, Fluor Corporation

"Put VPP Principles to Practice captures the essence of effective leadership that doesn't drive safety from the top down, but inspires safety from the bottom up, through empowering employees to build a zero incidents culture."
—David Jackson, Safety Manager of the Mission Support Alliance, and Chairperson of the VPPPA

"David Lynn's book Put VPP Principles to Practice is a giant step forward in understanding what it truly takes to establish safety excellence within an organization. You come away with a very clear understanding what it takes for an organization to attain and sustain an effective and proactive safety culture."
—Reginald Pitts, Regional Human Resources Director, GAF Corporation

"David has taken the approach that achieving excellence in safety and health is less about formality and more about truly leading and engaging employees to have ownership in their safety and health process to create the Win-Win for an organization. His use of personal experiences illustrates how safety and health becomes a way of life to help us create a culture of safety"
— Janet Nixon, VPP SME, Plexus Scientific Corporation

"Put VPP Principles to Practice is an excellent roadmap that would benefit any organization, whether large or small, in its successful implementation of the VPP elements. The steps are simple, easy to understand, and address the critical points necessary for expected results. David's knowledge of VPP, his professional experience in a variety of industries, and his insightful understanding of how to achieve results from individuals within the organization, makes this a "must read" book!"
— Bill White, Director of Operations, Fluor Operations & Maintenance

"The most successful safety professionals and organizations use proven approaches to achieve a zero incident culture. Putting VPP Principles to Practice will teach you how to do the same with confidence."

—Dave Walline, CSP, Global Safety Leader - Owens Corning

"Many publications on behavior safety and safe culture development are theory-based and provide little direction into 'how to' accomplish implementation. David lays out specific strategies, tasks, and timelines to practically work toward achieving implementation of an injury-free culture. Very refreshing."

—Ben Harris, Director, Environmental, Health, Safety & Security, Pick-n-Pull, a division of Schnitzer Steel Ind.

Principle to Practice

by David Lynn

FOREWORD
by Edwin G. Foulke, Jr.

For many decades and possibly even centuries, workplace safety and health has taken a back seat to production demands of the business. In the late '70s and early '80s, business had a preoccupation with quality and quality circles. At that time and continuing to the present, there has also been a strong focus on productivity and efficiency as companies utilized business tools such as Lean, Six Sigma, Just In Time, and 5S. Despite business' drive to improve the bottom line, most companies have continued only to provide lip service to safety and health in the workplace and, as a result, miss a tremendous opportunity to achieve increased profits.

As American businesses move into the new decade, the cost savings from productivity, efficiency and quality improvements have become smaller and smaller, more companies are looking for new areas of cost reduction in order to remain profitable and competitive in local, national or international level markets. For most companies there are two major areas where business cost savings can be achieved. Those areas are workers comp and health care. The only way business can tap into this potential cost savings is through safety. Based on these facts, I predict that, in the next decade, safety and health as well as safety and health professionals will play a predominant role in assisting companies to achieve greater competitiveness and profitability, thus keeping jobs here in America.

David Lynn, in his book Putting VPP Principles To Practice, focuses on those principles that will allow companies to remain competitive and profitable through safety. His analysis of the five principles necessary to have a comprehensive safety and health management system are the necessary building blocks for any company's successful safety program. These five principles, while assisting a company in achieving greater business success, also allows the company's employees to go home safe each and every night to their families and loved ones. Disappointingly, only a handful of companies have implemented these principles, but for those who have, the results have been substantial.

In this book, David Lynn examines the five principles for an effective safety and health management system, which include (1) management commitment; (2) employee involvement; (3) work site analysis; (4) hazard prevention and control; and (5) health and safety training. These five principles also form the basis for OSHA's Voluntary Protection Program ("VPP").

By examining the principles individually, Mr. Lynn details the steps necessary for successfully implementing each of these principles.

As a former Assistant Secretary of Labor for OSHA, I am well aware of the transformation that a company goes through by implementing the five principles. David Lynn discusses this transformation, which is nothing less than a culture change within the company and its employees. Surprisingly, once the employees recognize that management is seriously committed to having a safe and health work place and having the employees being actively involved in the program, a transformation occurs where the employees actually take ownership of safety and health as part of their daily job responsibilities. The cultural change is even further heightened when employees take this safety and health mentality to their homes and utilize it with their families. As a result, not only are work place injuries, illnesses and fatalities reduced substantially, which helps reduce the company's workers compensation cost but, at the same time, injuries and accidents at the home are also reduced, thus reducing the healthcare costs for employers. By following the roadmap outlined by David Lynn, an employer can substantially reduce its workers comp and healthcare costs, thus resulting in the company being more profitable and competitive. This in turn keeps more jobs in the company and within the country. Therefore, as businesses move into the next decade, safety and health is going to play a much greater role in allowing the company to remain profitable and competitive while at the same time improving the morale and retention of its employees. David Lynn's book could not be any more timely.

Edwin G. Foulke, Jr. - partner with Fisher & Phillips LLP, former Assistant Secretary of Labor for Occupational Safety and Health and the former Chairman of the Occupational Safety and Health Review Commission in Washington, DC.

Fisher & Phillips LLP
www.laborlawyers.com
Tel: (404) 240-4273

Acknowledgement

The inspiration to create a book comes from many perspectives, but the most important element I want to recognize is the desire to communicate lessons learned with a sense of personality. Safety is serious business, but we can communicate serious safety principles with a sense of humor. I hope my light-hearted approach to convey important messages will influence readers to apply these ideas in their environments.

Writing a book requires input from trusted sources, and I am blessed to have a group of highly qualified friends that volunteered to review my manuscript. I want to thank Christine de Vlaming for her eagerness to edit my material. She provided a valuable perspective from outside the safety profession. I would also like to show my appreciation for Dan Palmer's insight into the safety world. His experience and his skill to communicate safety ideas had an impact on the book. Sara Eschborn-Simmons also provided realism to the text that added value. Her input helped connect the content with the readers. And, Cheryl McNutt did a great job with the final edit. Cheryl's technical editing skills were critical to the final outcome of the book. I also want to thank Edwin G. Foulke, Jr. for reviewing the material and offering his words of wisdom in the Foreword. Everyone's positive approach to my request is an encouragement. They took the time to labor through the material, and they added incredible value to the project. Thank you all!

My family and friends have also provided unique inspiration that can be found in the analogies throughout the book. My boys Caleb, Jacob, and Luke offer a wealth of material to make safety relevant to a working environment. They teach me to look for critical safety messages in simple life experiences. I also want to recognize my wife Lisa. Her never-ending support made it possible to compile this work while never missing out on my family's adventures.

Some say that there is nothing new under the sun, but I think that there *is* always a unique experience in everyone's life that has the potential to impact another life. Our job is to share what we have seen, heard, and experienced, and I want to encourage readers to look for ways to improve the quality of life of those around them with their influence.

I also want to thank God for the influence He has had in my life and I want to thank Him for the opportunities He has given me that have inspired this book.

Put VPP Principles to Practice
Table of Contents

Foreword

Acknowledgement

Introduction

Put VPP Principles to Practice

Introduction

Safety reminds me of sports – it's all about fundamentals. Let me explain. When my nine year old son played baseball his first year, he had a lot to learn. Jacob's first season reminded me of how important a good coach is because a good coach will teach the fundamentals that make you successful. This was apparent when Jacob's little league team hosted a hitting clinic at a local batting cage. The owner of the batting cage taught Jacob more in 20 minutes than I could have taught him in years. The difference in the professional instructions and my advice was the level of detail and experience the coach possessed.

With my limited knowledge, I taught Jacob basic baseball principles. I focused on the obvious. Walk up to the plate. Get a good stance and swing the bat. If you make contact, run as hard as you can to first base. The principles were a good start, but Jacob did not have a concept of the basic technique. This lack of knowledge impacted his potential.

A good hitting coach enlightened both Jacob and me. He taught Jacob how to watch the ball and then he explained the purpose and consequence of every body position from the time a player approaches home plate until the time he walks back to the dugout. If you point the bat in the wrong direction in your stance, it affects bat speed. The way you balance your weight affects the power of your swing. The position of your head impacts the direction the ball will travel. The coach explained fundamental hitting techniques in slow- motion and with purpose. There is a cause and effect to every move. After he explained the fundamentals, each player demonstrated their technique as the coach fined tuned their skills. The coaching clinic was an awesome experience.

Does a good coach really make a difference? It did for my son Jacob! The fundamentals created consistency and Jacob began to build a foundation for success. But, the basics are not inherent to a nine year old boy's behavior. Somebody has to teach him, coach him, and encourage him so that he can adopt the behaviors that will make him a better player. Patience to train and a willingness to learn will build a cornerstone to success. Jacob is well on his way to becoming a fundamental baseball player.

Putting safety and health principles to practice takes a similar approach. You have to "know" that the basic principles of safety and health management are essential to success; principles like management commitment, employee involvement, worksite analysis, hazard prevention and control, and safety and health training – each of these basic principles not only make sense, they take into account everything we do in the name of safety and health. The principles of OSHA's Voluntary Protection Program (VPP) are similar to my approach in coaching my son Jacob. These principles help us to not only understand the rules of the game, but also to build a solid foundation upon which to add fundamental techniques that deliver consistent success.

I started my career learning safety **principles** through different jobs, but it took me several years to discover the right combination of techniques that creates a culture that embraces the belief that working with zero injuries is possible. Just like fundamental techniques for baseball are not inherent to nine year old baseball players, fundamental safety techniques are not inherent to safety professionals. I am proof of this fact. I learned fundamental safety techniques through unique and diverse job experiences.

I started my safety career in 1992, working for OSHA as a Compliance Officer. In this role, I conducted over 200 inspections ranging from scheduled audits to fatality investigations. My job with OSHA enabled me to see how the good and the bad companies managed safety across a wide variety of industries. The regulatory background taught me the rules. I also began to understand VPP principles on the surface, but I had no clue what it took to build a culture that believed you can work injury free. I thought the OSHA rules and generic VPP principles were the complete answer. I have learned that an injury free environment is more complex than I originally thought. An injury-free environment requires you to apply the rules and principles with disciplined techniques. The techniques allow you to apply your knowledge and build an injury-free work environment.

Although my OSHA experience did not teach me how to manage a safety program, knowledge of "the rules" enabled me to transition to a Safety Engineer's role at a plant that made alkaline batteries. The battery plant wanted OSHA experience and they got it when they hired me. My safety experience evolved in a fast-paced environment where the plant made over a billion batteries a year. For five years, I faced the challenge of leading injury prevention strategies with a large workforce in a high-demand industry. Through this role, I began to understand how important it is to translate regulatory requirements – "the rules" – into workplace habits that drive an injury-free culture. I wanted to enhance our safety culture, and I began to research opportunities to apply VPP principles. I knew VPP is a catalyst for improvement, but while I was at the battery facility, I could never get my arms around how to apply these principles in real-time fashion in a fast-paced industrial environment. My grasp of the general principles were not enough to put the initiative in motion.

In 2000, I accepted the challenge to work for another Fortune 500

Company as an Environmental, Health, and Safety (EHS) Manager. I was responsible for all environmental, health, and safety responsibilities during the construction phase of a state-of-the-art manufacturing facility. I also coordinated all EHS start-up requirements as the plant came on-line. Once the construction and start-up phase was complete, I remained the EHS Manager with the company until 2004.

The experience taught me that environments change. I learned how different phases of a project impact the way you lead safety. A construction environment has a unique personality with visible change on a daily basis. The site you see today isn't the same site you see tomorrow. Today there's a field, tomorrow a lay-down yard, and the next day your structure can emerge from the ground. You see the skyline change before your eyes. A start-up and commissioning phase creates unique hazards that are difficult to anticipate while a factory in operation has its own set of hazards and challenges.

Through experiences, I learned how to manage a safety and health program under dynamic circumstances, but I did not fully understand the importance of having a process that translated the principles into consistent action. I was like my son that went to the plate to bat without instructions from a qualified batting coach. I fully understood the principles of the game. I could stand at the plate, take a swing, and run to first base but my game lacked consistency and discipline. I did not understand the full cause and effect of the systems I implemented. I was a victim to the safety traps we all encounter – I searched for the latest and greatest "silver bullet" for safety performance.

In 2004, I accepted a position with Fluor Corporation as a Corporate Health, Safety & Environmental (HSE) Manager in Greenville, South Carolina. Fluor is one of the largest engineering, construction, and procurement companies in the world, with a distinguished safety reputation that the industry recognizes as one of the safest in the world. As a Fluor Corporate HSE Manager, I have supported HSE efforts in all of Fluor's Business Units. I witness incredible diversity in Fluor projects – power plants, refineries, roads, mines, chemical plants, and wide a variety of other projects. Fluor also performs maintenance in operating plant settings, each unique by its design and functionality. My experience at Fluor helped me "get it" to realize that safety and health management principles are universal, and that these principles are imperative. The ability to apply these safety and health principles WILL MAKE ONE SUCCESSFUL, without question, every time! Although it may take a while, it WILL HAPPEN!

The Fluor culture is built on VPP principles, and the principles are executed using fundamental techniques. At previous employers I learned the principles; but at Fluor, I witnessed how to apply these fundamental principles. The result is a culture that embraces the philosophy that you can work injury-free. The culture is confident. The expectations are high. The outcome is excellence.

The content of this book is based on what I have seen and heard in my career. I have been blessed with the opportunity to observe the good and the great, and I have tried to learn from my mistakes and build on my successes.

What have I learned through these diverse jobs?

Companies that excel in safety and health share common characteristics. They understand the fundamental safety and health principles, and they execute them through methodical techniques. Progressive safety leaders implement the five strategic principles of VPP: Management Leadership, Employee Involvement, Worksite Analysis, Hazard Prevention and Control, and Safety and Health Training.

This book is divided into five chapters that highlight OSHA's safety and health management principles for achieving VPP. Each chapter will discuss the value of the principle and then offer three techniques you can use to implement the principle. The techniques are a bridge to success. Principles only exist on paper until you make them a habit. Most crucial are the suggestions to implement the techniques. Compare the techniques to those in your safety and health program and prioritize which techniques you want to implement first.

With each technique, the section will offer suggestions to develop and implement the technique over a three-week period. This is a rapid delivery process that requires focus and commitment from your leadership team. The purpose of the three-week implementation is to establish a sense of urgency about change and improvement. Each week you will focus on a different element of the implementation. You will start with a planning phase with a team of employees. The second step will require you to communicate your strategy and in the third phase, you implement the process. The rapid delivery process works best when a core group of leaders understands the urgency and value of building an injury-free environment.

If you already use the technique, use the process to improve your current system. This book is a roadmap to build or enhance a culture that believes you can work injury-free.

Principle #1: Management Commitment

"Safety commitment does not exist without visible action."

Put your passion for safety into practice with visible commitment. Urgency, expectation, and discipline emerge from strong leadership. As a leader, every move you make has the potential to influence an injury free culture OR undermine the program you desire. The secret to building a winning culture begins with you! When individuals model a passion and conviction to achieve zero, organizations excel in safety. No matter where you fit in an organizational chart, you influence those around you. Your positive influence translates to a winning culture.

Leaders have to make their commitment visible. A commitment to safety is similar to a commitment to win in sports. You can see someone's competitive spirit, and their desire to succeed in how they respond to their environment. Leaders overcome obstacles and their confidence enables their success. They do what it takes to win; and they never accept loosing. Visible safety commitment projects an image that does not allow failure. Safety is not a recreational sport that you play for fun. With safety, you play to win!

I have polled thousands of employees over my career, ranging from employees on the shop floor to senior executives, and I discovered a consistent response. When I ask people, "Are you committed to safety?" One-hundred percent of the people raised their hands to confirm their commitment to safety. But, I ask you - how many people are REALLY committed to an injury-free work environment?

I have learned to follow my initial question with a more pointed question, "How do I <u>know</u> you are committed to safety?" My inquiry leads to a discussion about personal commitment through an individual's actions. A personal dedication to safety **does not exist** if one does not display the commitment with visible, consistent action. Your actions are a reflection of what you believe about safety.

You can make a difference. Everyone has the opportunity to demonstrate their dedication and their commitment to safety. Ask safety-related questions. Make positive safety suggestions. Offer safer solutions for your work area. Follow the rules. Learn everything you can about safety and teach others from your experience. Get excited and get involved with the safety process.

If you want to develop an injury-free culture, you have to do more than claim you are committed. You have to show your personal commitment with consistency that shows in your leadership. Raise your expectations, increase your urgency, and instill a disciplined approach to your management system.

Speak of safety
Players and fans love to relive wins and losses. If you love sports, you will talk about your sport in any environment, and your level of enthusiasm is a good indicator of how important the game is to you. Sports fans stand out because they will give you the play-by-play at home, at work, or in any casual setting. If it is important to you, you talk about it.

An employee with a heart for safety is like a big sports fan…everyone knows their commitment. The context of what you say and how you say it has the power to inspire people or, turn them off in a heartbeat. NEVER underestimate the power of your words, or your unspoken actions (nonverbal communication) – including body language! To impress safety on others, you must truly care about the quality of life of those around you. You have to truly believe that you can work injury-free.

You must motivate people with safety discussions. Talk about safety when you are on a break. Begin every meeting with a safety topic. Share influential safety experiences. True leaders inspire safety excellence and they develop a culture that expects and embraces safety excellence.

If an injury-free culture is important to you, it will naturally become a topic of your conversations, just like a sports fan talks about sports. Your challenge is to become safety's greatest fan and develop your injury-free culture, and relive the wins and losses every chance you get!

Actions (leadership) are a reflection of what people believe about an injury-free culture. No one will argue visible commitment is important, but you may ask, "How do I make my commitment visible?" I want to offer three techniques organizations can institute to visibly exhibit commitment. Each technique will take time to plan and prepare. I encourage you to make these three techniques a habit and communicate them from multiple directions. Your commitment **will not** exist without consistent and visible reinforcement of each technique.

Technique #1: Project Planning

To play to win, you have to have a game plan. Before my son Jacob took hitting lessons, he would go to the plate and swing the bat with little preparation or thought. After a significant amount of instruction, Jacob learned to think through his steps before he approached the plate. He watched the pitcher, he prepared his swing, and he thought through his technique. The game was the same, but the difference for Jacob was that he knew how to anticipate and prepare. He did not respond randomly. He thought through his actions, and that preparation enabled him to react to the pitch with precision.

A true injury-free culture applies visible management commitment through consistent methods of execution. In a basic but critical example, line management - with the assistance of the workers – must anticipate and plan each step. This preparation enables the work group to adjust to the unexpected and react with precision. You have to know how you will train the workers, analyze work, adapt to changing conditions, and control risks in all phases of the work. To the extent you can, you have to decide what you will do in each situation before you encounter the risk. Consistent planning, no matter the impacts on scope and schedule, will visibly show the workforce the level of commitment management places on planning for a safe and healthful outcome.

Mature safety cultures evaluate the nature of their jobs, and they put a plan in place to address the risk – every time. The time and energy spent dedicated to anticipate and mitigate risk is visible, especially to the workers. This visibility helps to cement a culture that recognizes safety is important. Recognition of this commitment creates a natural calmness and confidence in the workers, and they, over time, will come to expect a safe and healthy outcome, and will develop a correct discipline for safety.

To motivate confidence, dedicate time to anticipate worker needs before they occur; and above all, ask - no, INVOLVE - the experts, the workers! Make critical safety and health decisions upstream. Do not wait for a crisis to prompt you to plan. Anticipate the questions before they happen.

White-water rafting reminds me of the importance of anticipating risk. Once a year, I go to West Virginia to raft the New River or the Gauley River. Both rivers have class 4 and 5 rapids that command respect and test your courage. Because of the risk, we navigate the rivers with experienced guides. The guides sit in the back of the boat, and they coach us through every twist and turn. They anticipate the danger, and they explain the safest way to approach each rapid. The guides know how they will train rafters. They communicate critical safety points throughout the trip. They analyze the dynamic risk and they put controls in place to make the trip as safe as possible. If you listen to your guide, you stay in the boat. When you ignore their advice, you will take a bath in a giant wall of white water.

On one trip down the New River, our guide described an intense series of rapids. He told us how the river would zig and zag, and he explained how we could survive the boulders and walls of white water. He kept our attention as he warned us about undercut rocks with currents that will suck you to the bottom of the river. His urgent warnings also came with a backup plan. He pointed to where we needed to swim if we fell out of the boat, and he coached us on what to do if someone went overboard. My heart raced as I wondered if I would stay in the boat!

When we entered the rapids, we concentrated on the guide's instructions up until the moment the boat bounced one of our raft mates into the hydraulic abyss. Once overboard, he struggled to grasp the side of the boat while the river slammed him into the rocks. He needed help! We stopped paddling to pull him back in the boat. While we worked to pull him to safety, our guide continued to steer us through the danger. Our castaway slid back in the boat and everyone could feel his relief.

We survived the run down the river. Even though we dumped one person in the river, I know circumstances could have been worse if we did not have a guide who explained how to handle specific hazards before we reached the danger zone. He planned upstream. A good guide warns you of the dangers. He coaches you through the uncertainty. He instructs you in the midst of the current. He helps pull you to safety, and he ensures you get to the other side. I could not survive a trip down the New River without a guide.

The work environment is a dangerous place that also requires upstream preparation. Workers and managers in successful safety cultures develop a specific safety and health plan that helps the team execute work safely. They analyze the current of the work and they develop plans to get to the "other side." Successful safety cultures also develop backup plans for when work does not go as planned. These alternative plans help mitigate catastrophes. A thorough plan minimizes the pressure to take shortcuts that lead to injuries, and a comprehensive plan sets the safety expectations for the project. A good safety and health plan provides defenses for known hazards. A good plan also anticipates the unknown and answers questions before someone has to ask. A good rafting guide points to the danger downstream and instills the urgency to follow directions. Good safety leadership is the same. Take the next 21 days to develop and implement your plan.

I have three critical points of advice:
1. Don't get overwhelmed.
2. Don't make excuses.
3. No shortcuts.

Step 1 (week one)
Where does an organization start in the first week?
1. *Assemble a motivated Rapid Deployment Team (RDT).*
2. *Set the tone and plan with urgency.*
3. *Customize principles in this book to meet your demands.*
4. *Prioritize which techniques in the book you will implement first.*
5. *Decide how you will address training, hazard recognition, hazard control, visible commitment, and employee involvement.*
6. *Evaluate your risks and build your plan to address each risk, each hazard.*

Critical Implementation Point: *The RDT is successful when they build a safety plan to address a potential crisis.*

Step 2 (week two)
How do you communicate the plan in the second week?
1. *The RDT will develop a methodical communication strategy.*
2. *The RDT must communicate its intended approach to every person in a leadership position. Urgency, expectation, and discipline are the underlying tone.*

3. ALL elements of the plan, start dates, measurable goals, intent, and value must be communicated to the work group.

4. This is life or death and failure is not an option.

Critical Implementation Point: *Success means you never stop communicating the safety and health plan.*

Step 3 (week three)
How do you institute the plan in the third week?

1. Implement the top priority items in your plan.

2. Anticipate the challenges. Make it happen!

3. Measure and track your progress.

4. Meet weekly with your RDT to discuss progress.

Critical Implementation Point: *Nothing will happen until you convince those in positions of leadership of the value of your safety roadmap, your game plan, and your execution strategy.*

Technique #2: Measured Accountability

An exceptional game plan gives you the insight to win, but you don't KNOW who won without a score. The RDT has to build the scorecard for individual contributors. A strategic system to evaluate people will drive improvement and instill accountability. A score gives you a method to integrate urgency into an individual's daily expectations.

My three sons Caleb, Jacob, and Luke provide an example of the importance of keeping score. If I ask them how they are doing in school, what kind of response do you think I get? They communicate in one word sentences; good, fine, OK. What does that tell me? Does that give me a good description of their performance in school? No, it doesn't. If I want to know my boys performance in school, I have to look at their work. Every test has a score. Every project has a grade. Every report card has a final outcome. Their true performance is captured in their grades, and likewise, their grades reflect their effort. My urgency and expectations about their grades influences their performance. The rewards and consequences I provide for grades motivate my boys to perform, so I can't accept vague, general answers. I have to care about the details if I want Caleb, Jacob, and Luke to reach their potential. Weak safety cultures rely on inadequate responses to define safety success. When I worked with OSHA, I inspected over 200 sites and I experienced all kinds of inadequate descriptions of safety performance. When I asked sites to describe their safety performance, I received vague responses; fine, OK, good. Strong safety cultures avoid this trap; they keep score on critical "leading indicators," and they take an interest in the active details. Injury-free cultures do not accept generalities or mediocrity.

I think that we can all agree that "accountability" is essential for a successful safety and health program. But what does it mean to "hold" someone accountable for safety; and to "keep score" on their performance? This is often a deficient part of safety programs because leaders wait until something bad happens before they feel the need to hold anyone accountable. A negative event is too late to hold someone accountable for safety. The answer to accountability is simple: set standards for the people, measure the results, and either recognize or discipline based on the results. Do all this routinely and consistently.

For example, if audits are required, track audit participation and measure the quality of audits. If your organization values sustained corrective action, track the number of repeat observations on each audit. If your program requires supervisors to perform preshift safety meetings, track the quality and participation in the process. The records become a performance measurement. Tracking prompts rewards for achievement and consequences for failure to meet standards. True accountability means that if you do not meet your standard, you use progressive motivation – recognition or discipline – to drive desired results. Consequences can include termination. Remember, this is life or death. You cannot have a soft reaction for leaders that do not meet safety standards. The process of accountability provides for a perfect opportunity to instill expectations, urgency, and discipline into your program.

If your organization does not keep detailed individual scores for safety, you will experience an adjustment period when you introduce the idea. I learned this lesson the hard way. At a previous employer, I developed a scorecard that tracked management participation in four categories. I tracked audit participation, safety team support, safety meeting completion, and safety procedure reviews. Each supervisor and manager had responsibilities and I documented their performance. I gave them a score for each item and I rolled up the scores into a final score. Then, I stack-ranked each leader from the best to the worst. I highlighted the top ten percent in green and the bottom ten percent in red.

After the report was complete, I distributed the report to the leadership team. The process sounds reasonable...right? The score showed who followed through with their responsibilities and who did not. That is the type of accountability you need because it tells you who deserves a reward and who needs urgent "motivation," right? After all, safety is a condition of employment. You have to know the score and the score has to mean something, right? Yes to both questions, at least that's what I thought! Yes, well – others did not!

My plant manager was in the red! How do you hide your boss's poor performance? The system was awesome because it measured management commitment with visible tools that have been proven over time to drive safety success. Using this measurement method, one could not hide behind vague performance answers; good, fine, OK... The backlash was predictable. When my plant manager reviewed the results, he came to my office in a bad mood! Needless to say, he expressed his urgency with my approach. He was not happy and my scorecard had a short lifespan. Somehow, I managed to keep my job.

Where did I go wrong? Is scoring real safety performance bad? No, of course it's not bad. My mistake was I did not communicate the purpose and intent of the scorecard well, and I embarrassed important people. In reality, my plant manager always supported safety and I enjoyed working for him. But, I failed to properly explain the rules of the game. I did not provide enough communication to set the stage for a valuable measurement tool. That is a bad move and I learned from the experience. The moral of the story is you have to develop your scorecards as a team to gain the greatest value. Your team cannot fear the score. This is NOT an easy concept for all to embrace; in fact, this may be the toughest point of all. The goal, of course, is for leaders to embrace measurement techniques and play to win. The prize is a quality of life for your employees. Failure can be devastating, and thus, cannot be an option.

Another way to look at scorecards is to consider them an opportunity for you to demonstrate 360-degree leadership. In other words, you get an opportunity to lead all levels of the organization with your approach. You have a chance to influence your boss, mentor coworkers, and lead your employees by establishing the right criteria to measure. Once you have instituted the right measurements, you can train all levels of your organization on how to succeed in these areas. You give people the tools to lead safety. You show people how to become visible in the areas that count and this visibility builds your culture.

Since my initial scorecard experience, I have implemented similar systems with greater success. Buy-in from the appropriate parties was the key to success. Stack-ranking performance in critical safety systems identifies your weaknesses, and it sparks a sense of responsibility in those who do not want to finish in the red.

Use your scorecard for the following:

1. Improve your critical safety defenses.
2. Add teeth to your program. Give your expectations authority.
3. Use it as a tool to establish expectations, urgency, and discipline.
4. Recognize and reward high achievers; discipline, and even eliminate poor performers. If they cannot meet standards, do not allow them to lead. Do not allow poor performance.

Critical Implementation Point: In sports, coaches lose their jobs if they do not win. Your organization has to treat leadership performance in the same way, because winning with safety means that people do not get hurt.

SCORECARD

Step 1 (week one)
Where does an organization start in the first week?

1. *Assemble your RDT to develop your scorecard.*
2. *Choose three techniques with the greatest potential to drive performance.*
3. *Develop a scorecard that differentiates the good from the bad.*
4. *Set acceptable and unacceptable standards.*
5. *Determine what the uncompromised rewards and consequences are for personal scores.*

Critical Implementation Point: *Your accountability scorecard will succeed if you gain buy-in from your leadership team.*

Step 2 (week two)
How do you communicate accountability in week 2?

1. *The RDT will communicate the purpose and intent of the scorecard to all leadership employees.*
2. *Communicate the content of the plan, start dates, measurable goals, intent, and value.*
3. *The RDT will develop a methodical communication strategy to promote the scores.*
4. *Treat the scores like you would treat any other site measurement.*

Critical Implementation Point: *Leaders will not take the scorecard serious until they understand how you score their performance.*

Step 3 (week three)
How do you institute accountability in week 3?

1. *Measure your leadership performance in this phase.*
2. *Post the performance and recommunicate the process.*
3. *Use this period to coach slow learners and prepare them for the rewards and consequences.*
4. *Answer questions about how scores are calculated.*
5. *Managers should explain why employees are at the bottom of the list and help deficient employees put together a plan to improve.*
6. *Managers should have a serious "one-on-one" counseling session with all employees in the bottom ten percent each month.*

Critical Implementation Point: *Establish the authority of your scorecard with clear consequences for substandard performance and rewards for excellence.*

Technique #3: Strategic Visibility

Our Obsessions are Visible

You know when someone is obsessed with an idea or a hobby. When my boys Caleb, Jacob, and Luke were young, they wanted to be Super Heroes! They were obsessed with action heroes and their devotion to their favorite TV characters was unmistakable in everything they did and said. As they got involved with sports, they started obsessing over sports-related items. They covered their bedroom walls with sports posters and Jacob even slept with his football and kicking tee. He named his football after his favorite player. Each obsession is characterized by objects representing the obsession and attitude! You can't hide it because it is visible.

I think that we can all agree that my boy's obsession with super heroes and sports is innocent, but I think the greater question is, "What do WE as adults obsess over?" We demonstrate our level of interest in similar ways. Our thoughts are consumed by what is important to us. We surround ourselves with important "toys" and we finance our priorities. We imitate the people we admire and we take on the attitudes and actions of those we respect. Our interests are revealed through our personal obsessions, great and small! On the surface, I can tell people I am obsessed with safety and I feel better when I just repeat the words; but, do people around me *know* I am obsessed with safety? How would people describe my obsession? What safety costume do I wear, and what song do I sing? What safety attitude do I express through my behavior?

Our obsession with safety should be just as evident as my boy's obsession with super heroes and sports. Think about the value you will add to your coworker's quality of life if you become visibly fanatical about safety.

When is safety commitment real?

Safety commitment does not exist without visibility. The commitment becomes real when leaders develop obsessions about critical safety processes. Leaders can demonstrate their conviction in strategic ways. Where do you spend your time? The most critical point you need to remember about strategic visibility is that it does not have to cost money. Your presence in the right safety-related processes demonstrates what is important to you. Employees have to see your obsession!

For example, new employees form opinions in the first couple of hours they are on site. This is a perfect opportunity for site managers to set the safety tone by meeting with them. Take the opportunity to communicate safety expectations in person. Intentional interaction with employees during safety meetings, prejob meetings, and audits shows an employee safety is important to you. Ask safety-related questions. Workers know your interest by the questions you ask. When leaders balance management participation with decisive action, they visibly demonstrate safety is important.

Sample questions you can ask:
1. What are the critical steps in your job?
2. What is the worse thing that could happen?
3. How do you prevent the "worse" thing from happening?
4. How can I help you prevent a potential injury?
5. Do you feel like you get the proper safety training?

6. Do you feel like you get the proper instructions to perform tasks safely?

7. Do you feel comfortable stopping work if a hazard is present?

8. How do people around you demonstrate their commitment to safety?

9. Do you have the appropriate tools to complete your work safely?

10. Do you believe that all incidents (injuries, near misses, first aids, etc.) can be prevented?

11. Is there anything safety-related you would like for me to evaluate?

12. If you could make one safety improvement, what would you do?

Step 1 (week one)

Where does an organization start in the first week?

1. *Assemble your RDT and choose three strategic safety processes that need management visibility. (Example: audits, training, orientations, pre-planning meetings.)*

2. *Document what leaders should do when they participate.*

3. *Establish a schedule for participation. The schedule will identify who will go to which activities and how often.*

4. *Determine how you will track the participation.*

5. *Decide the positive rewards for participating and establish the consequences for not contributing to the schedule. (Example: include participation in awards and recognition programs.)*

6. *Include participation requirements in individual performance reviews.*

7. *Make consistent participation in established processes a condition of employment.*

8. *Initiate the schedule.*

Critical Implementation Point: There must be consequences for a lack of participation in this technique. Without rewards and consequences, the program will fail.

Step 2 (week two)

How do you communicate the plan in the second week?

1. *Continue to communicate the concept of visible commitment.*
2. *Talk about safety visibility in every possible setting.*
3. *Communicate why it is important, talk about the benefits of visibility, confirm your desired outcome, relate your personal experiences, and define success.*

*Critical **Implementation Point**: Leaders want practical reasons for why their visible activities add value. Reinforce the message and communicate the purpose.*

The benefits include: a) you establish relationships with your employees; when people trust you, they are more willing to follow your leadership; b) visibility gives you an opportunity to show you are on the same team; people can't tell if you are sincere about your commitment until you show them; and c) visibility also offers you an opportunity to identify risk and correct hazards.

Step 3 (week three)

How do you institute the plan in week three?

1. *The RDT has established expectations. You have delivered the communication in multiple venues. Leaders have initiated their action.*
2. *Monitor progress to ensure leaders follow through with their commitment to visibility.*
3. *Report on the visibility status in daily meetings. Make everyone's visibility or lack thereof transparent.*
4. *Have leaders share what they have learned from their interaction with employees.*
5. *Follow-up on items that require corrective action.*
6. *After three weeks, assemble the RDT and discuss the impact. Compile information about what you have learned and build on your success.*

Critical Implementation Point: Establish the expectation for strategic visibility, communicate the value, monitor progress, and follow through relentlessly.

Summary Principle 1 – Management Commitment

Visible management commitment is the cornerstone to success, and it is a mark that distinguishes a culture. I wish everyone committed to safety had a green ear. Would that not make life easier? If you faced a complicated safety issue, you would know who could give you sound safety direction. You would know exactly who to count on for keeping people safe in your work environment. A distinguishing mark could indicate everyone's safety expectations. On the flip side of the coin, you would also know exactly how to identify people who are not engaged in safety. People with a green ear represent commitment and they could influence those without a green ear.

Unfortunately, physical features can't outwardly reveal safety commitment, but visible consistent behaviors measure a commitment to safety. Our words and actions project our commitment, and we have to ask ourselves difficult questions requiring honest reflection on our approach to safety. These reflections are important to discovering a true commitment to safety. All of our actions represent a footprint for safety, and we project an image whether we like it or not. How would your coworkers describe your focus on safety? Do you have a green ear for safety? You may not come to work with a green ear, but you have opportunities every day to demonstrate you believe an injury-free culture is possible.

Principle # 2 - Employee Involvement

"Safety is more than a number. It is all about people."

Are your employees just a number? People want to work for employers that see and treat them as individuals and not as a statistic. Workers want to spend their eight plus hours a day with coworkers who care. Safety metrics are always important, but to build an injury-free culture, ask, "How do I visibly put people first? Am I building mutual respect?" When the focus shifts from a number to a person, safety initiatives gain value - and a sense of urgency. This encourages people to take ownership of safety, and to become involved since (among other reasons) they now see themselves as "owners." Sincere ownership and involvement promotes safety success; in fact, many will suggest that we can't have "true" success without employee ownership and involvement!

A Player's Coach

Every coach wants to win. They have an intense focus on the "numbers" that represent victory, but successful coaches do more than win on the scoreboard. They take a personal interest in their players and develop relationships with them. With a coach's genuine leadership, players and coaches build a mutual respect for each other. That admiration enables a positive culture with the potential to win on and off the field. Players never forget their coaches, and they perform harder for a "players' coach" because there is more to the game than the score. There is a mutual respect and admiration.

Make safety personal by building relationships with those around you and take advantage of opportunities to learn what is important to your coworkers. Adopt a servant's heart that has a desire to help people. When you make other's needs a priority, you will be amazed at how it changes your perspective towards safety. Each number begins to represent someone's best friend, spouse, or parent.

A players' coach recognizes the value of the relationship with his players. Building a winning safety culture requires the same focus — a focus that values the faces behind the numbers.

Walk in Someone Else's Shoes

I have a friend – "Jeff" - who works as a maintenance operator at a paper mill. When I want to check my "people" focus on safety, I like to consider how I would deal with particular situations if Jeff was involved. I respect Jeff's opinion, as it is based on years of experience; and I know if I am making decisions that would cause Jeff heartburn, I am on the wrong path. For example, when I manage workers' compensation cases, I like to imagine how I would handle the situation if Jeff was the injured employee. I want to treat people as though they were a good friend. If I am implementing or enforcing a safety policy, I will give it the "Jeff test" to keep my focus on people. I want my decisions to be based on methods that make sense to the people that have to live with them. This is one portion of employee involvement that we do not often consider. But it will influence how you make decisions, because the object of your choices will be about people – not numbers.

Trust and Respect

People respond better to leaders they trust and respect. Trust and respect come from the relationships you build in your work environment. You have to earn these qualities – but rest assured, they have a powerful impact in your work environment.

How do you know if you have earned the trust and respect of employees at work? Is work a dreaded place, or do you find enjoyment in accomplishing goals with the people you work with every day? How do you describe your day at work? Did you avoid people, or do you build relationships with those you interact with at work? Our attitude and outward demeanor subtly dictates our safety performance. For example, if we find a way to get along with those around us, and if we enjoy their company, safety takes on new meaning. You are more eager to work together and prevent each other from getting hurt when you actually like each other! A positive attitude and regular cooperation will do wonders for your safety culture. Hiding behind the aisles at work to avoid people does not create a positive climate for eliminating risk and unsafe behavior.

Technique #4: Safety Champion

A safety champion identifies risk and addresses issues. Find champions for your program and use their leadership abilities to monitor safety. Build relationships with the natural leaders at work and you can earn their trust and respect.

How do you identify the right people? It is really not difficult. Safety-minded employees are impressive, and you can't mistake who they are, because you can see the fruits of their labor. If you observe someone who is safety-conscious, you will notice that they take their safe attitude everywhere they go. They cannot complete a task without considering the consequences. They know what hazards to look for and find a way to reduce risks. What is even more impressive is they boldly share their safety-related views with the people they work with every day. They do not worry about how people will perceive their message, because they know that safety is a personal responsibility and they encourage people around them to work safer.

Safety-minded employees are not perfect but they do have a desire to learn, and they want to influence coworkers in the safest direction. Even a shy person can make a difference in safety when they accept responsibility for helping those around them. Safety-minded employees overcome their fears of confronting people about unsafe behavior and they learn to approach safety with a helpful attitude and encouraging tone.

The key to a successful Safety Champion Program is not the depth of the employee's safety knowledge but rather their willingness to positively influence those around them.

What is a Safety Champion Program?

A Safety Champion Program identifies natural leaders on the jobsite, and gives them the responsibility to focus on safety in their work area while still performing their assigned duties. Safety champions become an advocate for safety and they monitor safe behavior and conditions in their area. They provide a positive peer-to-peer influence with other employees.

I introduced the idea at a former employer. The facility had approximately 1100 employees and operated seven days a week, twenty-four hours a day. It was a fast-paced environment with a lot of ground to cover, and I struggled to involve a cross section of the organization in our safety processes. I was faced with the questions, "How do I get people meaningfully involved with safety? How do I help people feel like they are more than a number? How do I include the right number of people across seven days and multiple shifts?" I was only one person!

I chose to use a Safety Champion Program and I selected representatives from each department and all shifts to participate in the program. I wanted to develop leaders, not followers, because I knew leaders would influence more people. At least 75 employees participated in the program. Each supervisor selected two natural leaders to participate. This gave us a primary participant and an alternate from each work group.

The goal was to use the champions to help coach, mentor, and assess risk in their areas. The champions became advocates for safety that people on their shift would come to with questions and suggestions. Each champion was responsible for conducting a peer-to-peer safety assessment each week in their area; they would assess standard requirements that included behavior-based elements as well as condition-oriented expectations. To support the program, I met with the champions on each shift once a week to coach and mentor. At each session, we discussed the observations and the obstacles they faced during the peer-to-peer assessments. The communication process was a two-way street. I would also invite managers and supervisors to the meetings so that they could show their support to the program. In such a large and diverse environment, this approach offered a consistent venue for managers and employees to meet and discuss the direction of our safety performance. We also rotated different people through the Safety Champion Program to expose more members of the facility to the process.

The Safety Champion Program was a success. The key is to select the right people and give them specific tasks that they have control over. Constant communication and support is also an important element to make the process work. Make the opportunity to serve on the safety champion team a privilege and stress the importance of each member encouraging others in the workforce. Reward such service in some tangible way.

Step 1 (week one)
Where does an organization start in the first week?

1. Assemble your RDT and decide what qualities you are looking for in safety champions.

2. Determine how many champions you want. It is important to have a general idea, but don't let the "required number" force you into choosing people who do not meet your qualifications. If you have to start with just a few people that meet your criteria, do so.

3. Build on your core group of champions. The process relies on leadership.

4. Interview your potential champions. This can give the program significance.

5. Select your champions. Make it an honor to participate.

Critical Implementation Point: Do not put anyone on the safety champion team that has a remotely negative attitude. They will poison the group.

Step 2 (week two)
How do you communicate the plan in the second week?

1. Let your champions know you chose them to participate.

2. Communicate their responsibilities.

3. Promote the process in your facility.

4. Make sure supervisors and managers get to know the champions. (Example: Feed them lunch, visit them in their work area, communicate their participation in meetings, and other miscellaneous venues.)

5. Make the safety champions visible to the workforce. (Example: Posters, video, etc.)

Critical Implementation Point: It will take time for employees to build trust in the Safety Champion Program. People respond to positive results. Plan your strategy to communicate successes in the Safety Champion Program.

Step 3 (week three)
How do you institute the plan in the third week?

1. Train your safety champions. Explain expectations and responsibilities.

2. Deliver the information they need to perform their jobs.

3. Walk through the observation process with the safety champions.

4. Have the safety champions perform a trial run.

5. Begin collecting information from the safety champions.

6. Meet with the safety champions as a group and discuss the progress with the trial run.

Critical Implementation Point: It will take time for your safety champion team to settle into their roles. Remain patient and work through the transition by giving your team a cause to work towards.

Technique #5: Employee Mentoring

An employee mentor teaches new employees to do their jobs safely. You can't learn how to do your job in the classroom! You accumulate useful knowledge listening to an instructor, but you learn the practical hands-on functions of your job from those you work with every day. On-the-job training is a natural part of everyone's learning process. An employee peer-to-peer mentoring process utilizes trusted employees to develop positive safety attitudes and disseminate critical information to new employees. This is similar to a Safety Champion Program but the difference is the mentor's focus. The mentor focuses on training new employees in their first 30 days while the Safety Champion Program focuses on monitoring behaviors and conditions throughout the life of the job.

When I started work as a Compliance Officer at OSHA in 1992, I spent the majority of my first four months in a room the size of two cubicles with four other people. The objective was to study OSHA standards! We did this every day for four months! Can you imagine spending eight hours a day, five days a week trapped in a small room staring at the Code of Federal Regulations? How exciting is that? Better yet, how effective is that?

The training was not an orientation but rather an initiation. I don't know how much I learned the first four months in my OSHA role, but I – along with my coworkers – survived the imprisonment. The next stage of the program was MUCH more useful. We shadowed experienced Compliance Officers on their inspections, and I began to see how people did the job I would learn to do. The experienced Compliance Officers were my mentors and they taught me the hands-on details of the job. That is where I really learned the most. Over the next 9 months, I learned every facet of the inspection and report writing process with a mentor. As I progressed, the Compliance Officers would let me do more of the job. It was an incremental process that taught me the details. After a year, I passed a final evaluation and began performing inspections solo.

The lesson I learned in my OSHA experience is that "book learning" is important - but it is not where you learn how to do your job. You learn your job from people. Companies with a history of exceptional safety performance have systems that take advantage of the power of peer-to-peer learning. Give safety-minded employees an opportunity to instill their safety values into new employees via mentoring. This helps perpetuate a culture that embraces safety.

An effective mentoring program should accomplish specific goals. The program should identify safety-conscious leaders in your workforce. The program should offer an opportunity to train the mentors. The mentors should evaluate and coach new employees. Then, the mentors can then evaluate the new employee's safety awareness after a predetermined time. The goal is to add structure to the way employees learn to do their jobs and empower employees to train new people.

Step 1 (week one)
Where does an organization start in the first week?
1. *Assemble your RDT to map out your game plan for implementation.*
2. *Research the statistics for how often employees get hurt in the first 90 days of employment. Use site- company-, and industry-specific data. Use whatever is available to make your case.*
3. *As a team, decide what qualities you want in a safety mentor.*
4. *Determine how many mentors you would like to have.*
5. *Interview your potential mentors. This can give the program significance.*
6. *Select your mentors. Identify ways to make it an honor to participate.*
7. *Decide how you will train mentors. Discuss the material you will use and the schedule for training.*
8. *Develop a simple checklist for evaluating new employees. Mentors will use the checklist to confirm new employees understand the safety cultural expectations.*
9. *Decide how long the mentor will take to mentor and evaluate the employee. Recommendation: Mentors should take a minimum of 30 days to coach and encourage new employees. After 30 days, the mentor can*

complete the form.

10. *Determine how you will track progress and define success in the system.*

11. *During this phase, also consider how you may institute the mentoring with different types of employees. For example in a construction environment, an employee may be on site for a short period of time. You will have to take the concept of mentoring and find a way to apply it to a short term environment.*

Critical Implementation Point: *Don't put anyone in a mentoring position that has a remotely negative attitude. They will poison the group.*

Step 2 (week two)
How do you communicate the plan in the second week?

1. *Notify your mentors and begin to give them ownership of the safety performance of new employees. The mentors need to feel responsible for the safety of the new employees.*

2. *Provide mentors with training that defines their responsibilities and explains the expectations.*

3. *Make sure your leaders get to know the mentors.*

4. *Management needs to visibly show their commitment to the program by talking with mentors on a regular basis.*

5. *Make the mentors visible to the workforce.*

6. *Promote the Safety Mentoring Program throughout your facility with all available mediums (newsletters, bulletin boards, meetings, posters, etc.).*

7. *Communicate the value of the program by stressing the urgency to protect new employees. Experienced employees are the natural answer to establishing a hedge of protection around new employees.*

8. *The idea is to turn the problem over to your workforce and let them become the solution.*

9. *Help people understand that new employees are at risk and coworkers have to train them properly. The process has to be visible, and you have to give people a cause to rally around.*

Critical Implementation Point: *Plan your strategy to communicate successes in the Safety Mentoring Program. You have to highlight the difference people make.*

Step 3 (week three)
How do you institute the plan on the third week?

1. *Assign a mentor to all employees who have worked in your facility less than 90 days*
2. *Introduce mentors to your employees and explain the purpose behind the program.*
3. *Allow mentors the opportunity to meet with the new employees and interact with them.*
4. *Have mentors review the scoring criteria on the checklist with employees.*
5. *Allow mentors to take new employees on a tour of appropriate areas and discuss safety expectations.*
6. *The RDT should meet with safety mentors at the end of the three weeks and discuss what will add value to the program.*
7. *The RDT and the mentors will have to find the right niche to make the process work.*
8. *Consistent and methodical communication between the mentors and managers will enable the process.*

Critical Implementation Point: *To succeed, the Safety Mentoring Program cannot loose site of the primary purpose of the program. You have to empower peer-to-peer learning through a formal process, and leaders have to constantly nurture the program.*

Technique #6: Safety Perception Surveys

Perception is reality! But whose perception is the reality? The landscape from a cruising altitude of 37,000 feet will give you a unique perspective on the world. When you fly over the Midwest, you notice how the scenery is divided into squares as far as the eye can see. The boundaries of each square are designated by fence lines, irrigation systems, roads, crop lines, and unique topography. The borders are straight as an arrow and crystal clear. These squares paint a picture of a giant checker board with a farm house sitting in the corner of the board. As the plane descends, your perspective changes because you no longer see the checkerboard. The boundaries still exist, but you are unable to mark their presence. Your organization's culture has a similar "bird's eye" view, and it is important to understand the boundaries and obstacles from a cruising altitude. Safety Perception Surveys can help identify the checkerboard in your organization. You can also use the surveys to canvas the opinion of different levels of the organization and compare the difference.

At this lower altitude, your perspective changes. You experience the obstacles first hand, on a day-to-day basis. Consider how the ground-level view impacts the success of your program, and assess whether there is a difference? How does your organization's safety culture appear from a cruising altitude of 37,000 feet compared to a ground-level perspective? Both views are important because they give you a strategic perspective as well as a real life idea of the obstacles and barriers to building your safety culture. The point is, if you sit in an office you will have a different opinion than people on the shop floor. You may have a strong handle on the procedural and organizational side of safety, but the safety in the field may reveal a different reality. The two perspectives need to work together to create a total picture.

The working landscape is riddled with boundaries and obstacles that hinder us from achieving an injury-free culture. Misperceptions, lack of understanding, and apathy towards an injury-free culture represent attitudes that will hurt your efforts to build a strong program. To move forward, you have to know how employees and managers perceive safety. The two different perspectives reveal the barriers. Challenge your organization to get a bird's eye view as well as a ground-level view of what makes your program tick.

Use simple Safety Perception Surveys on a quarterly basis to solicit input from your workforce as well as your management. The information IS important – but your response to the information is critical. What do you do with the input? You analyze the results; identify the weaknesses; research why people feel the way they do; put a plan in place to improve the perception.

Step 1 (week one)

Where does an organization start in the first week?

1. *Assemble your RDT to define your survey strategy.*

2. *Discuss the purpose and value of the process.*

3. *Develop your survey questions using 5 categories: 1) Management Commitment 2) Employee Involvement 3) Worksite Analysis 4) Hazard Prevention and Controls 5) Training and Education.*

4. *Craft 5 questions per category. Ask your audience questions that will help you understand the level of respect and value the audience has for the critical category.*

5. *Establish the implementation strategy. The strategy should include how you will pole your workforce, collect the data, analyze the results, and address trends.*

Critical Implementation Point: *The success of the Safety Perception Survey process is contingent on the team's ability to ask the right questions and respond appropriately to the trends.*

Step 2 (week two)

How do you communicate the plan in the second week?

1. *Communicate through all appropriate venues that you want to know what people think about safety.*

2. *Utilize your safety champion and safety mentor network to push your message to people. Their opinion is important.*

3. *Distribute the survey to all employees.*

4. *Collect the information and track your response percentage.*

5. *Perform a trend analysis on the data.*

6. *Compare the difference between the management perception and the general workforce perception.*

7. *Communicate the results to everyone.*

Critical Implementation Point: *Make the Safety Perception Survey process transparent. To get legitimate data, people will have to feel the process generates a positive response.*

Step 3 (week three)

How do you institute the plan in the third week?

1. *Assemble a team of employees to analyze the results.*

2. *Choose the top three trends and determine what is driving the trends.*

3. *Put together a plan to improve the weak areas.*

4. *Meet with the team regularly to follow-up on the action plan.*

5. *Measure progress with another survey the next quarter.*

Critical Implementation Point: *For the Safety Perception Survey to succeed, you have to distribute the survey to a wide audience, identify the trends, acknowledge the drivers, and address the weak portions aggressively.*

Summary Principle 2 – Employee Involvement

Everyone has to participate and take ownership of safety in a mature injury-free culture. That is why employee involvement is such a critical part of OSHA's VPP program. I have witnessed OSHA representatives interview 50 percent of a workforce to gauge the level of employee participation. They take employee involvement serious because they know it has a huge impact on safety performance.

Employee involvement with safety reminds me of sports. You have spectators and you have players. Avid fans enjoy observing the game, but players have the ultimate fulfillment because they make the sacrifices necessary to win. Strong safety cultures get people involved and they make the sacrifices necessary to win. Just like players benefit from the outcome of a game, employees benefit from their efforts to achieve safety excellence. Imagine a work environment where management enables each employee to participate in the game. The potential for safety excellence is unlimited. To create an injury-free culture, organizations groom players with a drive to win. Organizations finally begin to achieve their potential when their workforce becomes unsatisfied as a spectator, and they step on the field to compete.

The goal for this section is to offer three suggestions for how you can transition spectators into players in your work environment. With safety champions, mentors, and surveys, you can offer meaningful ways for people to get involved. The processes cultivate a spirit of engagement and it helps develop a desire to win in your organization.

Principle # 3: Worksite Analysis

"Injury prevention starts with risk perception."

"I'm from Corporate and I'm here to help!" In a previous job, I had the privilege of hosting my share of environmental, health, and safety auditors. Doesn't that sound like fun? On one occasion, our corporate office even scheduled audit training at our facility, and we hosted 25 eager participants. They would spend half of the day in the classroom learning to be ruthless inspectors, and then they would spend the rest of the day implementing their probing tactics. What a "joyful" week! I survived the intense week, but I found it hard to feel like they were there to help.

I have also experienced audits from a corporate and regulatory role. I have traveled to projects and used those fun loving words, "I'm from corporate and I'm here to help." I have approached the responsibility with humility, because I've been on the other side of the fence. I have tried hard _not_ to be the stereotypical "corporate helper." Three primary sources have prompted my visits. The most urgent type of request involves an incident requiring immediate attention. In such a case, I assist the project with a thorough investigation and assessment to help them move forward. The second type of request involves projects having difficulty meeting performance objectives. An assessment is done to help them achieve their goals. This is a boost to get past certain hurdles. The third kind of request generally comes from project leaders who are meeting their goals, but have a sincere desire to do better. They want to enhance their program performance. Each request comes from a position of need, but the needs take on different forms and attitudes.

From which position would you prefer to request help? Despite the circumstance, I identify the appropriate set of requirements/standards, and compare and measure against that set of standards. From the comparison, we map out recommendations to move forward and improve. The process is met with a variety of responses. Some managers disagree; some leaders grit their teeth and respond reluctantly; and some leaders take the information and recognize the opportunity to do a better job. Circumstances always influence the mood of an assessment; but depending on the heart of the leader, actions and progress may vary substantially. The leader may have perceptions filled with mental barriers – or filled with hopeful excitement!

Let me ask you – where is your heart for improvement today? Do you disagree with suggestions? Do you proceed with reluctance? Or, do you have a genuine desire to do better and plan for success? The state of your heart for improvement – to a large extent – will very likely dictate your future safety performance, and the plan of attack that you adopt for improvement. Take an objective look at your safety program and overall plan. To be sure of successful pursuit of genuine improvement, pursue excellence with a willing heart.

In this section, we will describe common techniques every site should apply in a way that works best for your environment. The secret to success is each employee's attitude toward identifying and correcting hazards. Adopt an attitude that accepts each analysis tool as an opportunity to improve.

Technique #7: Field Audits

You have to audit your processes. I remember my first job after I graduated from college because that job made people uncomfortable. I was amazed at how people became so nervous when I introduced myself. I was only 23 years old – how could I intimidate people? I guess they were nervous because I was an OSHA Compliance Officer and "I was there to help" – if you know what I mean. After all, doesn't everyone want an unannounced visitor from the Department of Labor?

The irony of my job with OSHA is – I was 10 times more nervous than the people I inspected. I am nonconfrontational and introverted. I don't like to identify a stranger's problems. Even after more than 200 inspections, the nervousness never went away. Even though the anxiety never subsided; I became more confident in my job because I learned the OSHA standards and how they applied. I learned how to interact with people and answer their questions with self-assurance. When I did not have the answer, I knew where to get them. Overall, the experience and repetition made my job easier.

As you develop your audit program, participants will gain confidence with experience and repetition as well. Listed below are six elements that will make your field audit program successful:

1. **Participation is vital.** Anyone who supervises or directs employees should conduct audits appropriate for their area of responsibility. When leaders support the audit program with their participation, they instill a sense of urgency in the program and their presence should drive corrective action.

2. **Audit frequently.** Participants should perform audits every week. There is more value in frequent short audits than long drawn out audits because people accumulate expectations. They know if you look for risk on a regular basis, it prompts them to prepare – if you audit less frequently, preparation is less frequent. The bigger risk, the more

you should assess the risk.

3. **Participants have to develop confidence with their audits.** Leaders drive the success of the audit program with their confidence in their ability to identify and correct safety observations. When I started with OSHA, I was nervous for two reasons: 1) I did not know what to look for in most environments. 2) I have a reserved personality. I overcame both obstacles with experience. I built on the knowledge I gained at each site I visited. Coach and encourage participants and allow them the opportunity to learn how to identify risk and confront the issues.

4. **Identify standards to which you will audit.** What if OSHA did not audit to a preselected set of standards – what if OSHA had the authority to make rules up as they go from site to site? As the one being audited, you would never know how to prepare. So, give people an opportunity to succeed – tell them what you will look for each time you conduct an audit.

5. **Follow through with corrective actions.** Document all observations – be sure you have explained clearly what the issues and non-compliances are; then, monitor corrective actions. Keep in mind that long-term true corrective actions eliminate hazards. If you correct it today and it resurfaces tomorrow, is it really corrected?

6. **Hold leaders accountable!** If you expect a certain level of performance, do not let people perform less without consequences. Record, track, and eliminate repeat observations – then reward those who do well. A good audit program is a great tool to see who has what it takes to influence and lead. If one can't manage safety, one can't manage the rest of the business effectively.

You have to give people a chance to perform well. But when people fail to perform, you have to take aggressive action. When my sons were eight, six, and four, they shared the same room. You can imagine how clean their room looked. One Saturday I decided to correct the problem. I put them in their room and pointed out the mess. I gave them suggestions on how to neaten their disaster zone.

I told Caleb, Jacob, and Luke they had one hour to clean their room. If they passed my inspection, they could come out of their room. If they did not clean their room in one hour, I promised them I would clean it my way.

They whined and disagreed for a solid hour and they did not accomplish one thing! So, I was true to my promise. I went into their room to clean my way. I packed trash bags full of toys and took them away. All three boys wailed with dissatisfaction, "Daddy, don't throw our toys away." I had one response, "You should have done what I asked."

Their room stayed clean after that. And no, I didn't throw their toys away! After all, the punishment DOES have to fit the crime. But it WAS several weeks before I gave the toys back to my boys. The moral of the story is that at some point, you stop asking and you start administering consequences. The key is to make sure people understand that there is a limit to how long noncompliance or inaction will last before there are consequences. My boys could have cleaned their room in ten minutes and enjoyed their Saturday. They learned from the experience.

Step 1 (week one)
Where does an organization start in the first week?

1. Assemble your RDT to define your strategy.

2. Determine who will perform audits and how often.

3. Define which areas you will audit.

4. Develop site-specific standards you will audit.

5. Create a scorecard for your audit so that you can track improvement.

6. Determine rewards and consequences for good and bad performance.

Critical Implementation Point: Keep your audit program simple; consistency in your audit program is more important than complexity.

Step 2 (week two)
How do you communicate the plan in the second week?
1. *Train participants. Explain the expectations and philosophy.*
2. *Teach participants how to make observations.*
3. *Explain your scoring system.*
4. *Perform pilot walk-through audits to confirm comprehension.*
5. *Communicate the rewards and consequences for scores.*

Critical Implementation Point: *Over-communicate the standards you will audit.*

Step 3 (week three)
How do you institute the plan in week three?
1. *Perform your audits.*
2. *Allow people to work in pairs.*
3. *Auditors should walk through areas with the area owner.*
4. *Review observations with the area owner.*
5. *Take pictures of good and bad observations.*
6. *Assemble the RDT after all audits are complete and review pictures.*
7. *Use pictures for future training.*
8. *Track corrective action. Have area owners sign off on completed items.*
9. *Track repeat items and reward good performers for eliminating repeat items. Administer consequences for unacceptable repeat items.*
10. *Communicate results and trends with all employees. Make the process visible.*

Critical Implementation Point: *The ultimate audit program eliminates repeat findings. Give the audit program teeth with rewards and consequences.*

Technique #8: Self-Assessments

What is a self-assessment? How is it different from a field audit? A self-assessment is conducted by "you." Similar to an audit, a self-assessment is a systematic, documented, and objective review comparing how you comply with your management system (your policies and procedures) and regulatory requirements. A self-assessment measures effectiveness with field execution as well as administrative requirements. Self-assessments are system tools, and the process encourages sites to evaluate administrative controls. They establish consistency and they offer an opportunity for employees to learn the management system in depth.

Growing up, our family had built-in health care – my mother was a nurse. My brother and I experienced a full range of sicknesses and injuries, but Mom could handle anything. If we were sick, she knew what medicine to give us. If we were hurt, she gave us a Band-Aid. An unplanned doctor's visit meant there was a serious problem because Mom could diagnose and treat most problems.

Even though unplanned doctor's visits were rare, my brother and I knew that we still had to suffer through an annual physical at the pediatrician. I never understood why Mom would not take us to the doctor when we were sick but with out fail, she would take us for that annual physical when we felt fine! How does that make sense?

I guess if you are sick, the symptoms are obvious and the treatment is standard. Why go to the doctor just so he can tell you, "you are sick - take two aspirin and call me in the morning." Mom could do that without getting out the checkbook. An annual physical is different. The doctor would poke and prod to look for the hidden problems. Your blood work and various samples reveal internal conditions. The annual physical looks beyond superficial signs.

The difference between field audits and self-assessments is similar to treatment for minor aches and pains verses a comprehensive checkup. A field audit requires you to walk through an area and make observations during a specific time. If you don't see anything, all is well. A comprehensive self-assessment requires that you assess and verify elements of your management system. You take procedures and evaluate their effectiveness and then you take the procedure to the field to verify people follow the procedure. A systematic approach to checks and balances within your system will gage the internal health of your program. The assessment and verification process is like blood work at the doctor – it reveals the hidden dangers.

Step 1 (week one)
Where does an organization start in the first week?
1. *Assemble your RDT to define your strategy.*
2. *Determine who will assist with the assessment.*
3. *Develop a site-specific protocol for your assessment.*
4. *Create a scorecard for your audit so that you can track improvement.*

Critical Implementation Point*: Know your management system and assess the effectiveness with a team.*

Step 2 (week two)
How do you communicate the plan in the second week?
1. *Train participants. Explain the expectations and philosophy.*
2. *Teach participants how to make observations and verify compliance.*
3. *Explain your scoring system.*

Critical Implementation Point*: Over-communicate the standards you will assess and use a team approach to your annual assessment.*

Step 3 (week three)
How do you institute the plan in the third week?
1. *Perform your assessment.*
2. *Allow people to work in pairs.*
3. *Auditors should observe and verify compliance with field and adminis-*

trative requirements.

4. *Review observations with the area owner.*

5. *Assemble the RDT and review findings.*

6. *Track corrective actions. Have area owners sign off on completed items.*

7. *Communicate results and trends with all employees. Make the process visible.*

Critical Implementation Point: *The ultimate audit and assessment program eliminates repeat findings and it is a teaching tool.*

Technique #9: Incident Investigations

Why did it happen? When I worked with OSHA as a Compliance Officer, I performed several fatality investigations. I remember assisting a Compliance Officer with one of my first fatality investigations and it involved a fatality in a grain silo. The silo had an auger in the bottom of the silo that transported corn. The corn had formed a crust over the auger and prevented the flow of corn. Two teenage cousins went into the silo to shovel the corn to another opening in the side of the silo. They had to walk on top of the 15 foot pile of corn to perform their job in the silo. While they moved the grain to the side opening, they dislodged the corn above the bottom auger. As the corn began to funnel through the bottom auger, the flow created a whirlpool effect and the boys could not escape. It was like they were stuck in quicksand. They screamed for help but the response was too slow. One boy stood on a board on top of the corn holding his cousin's hands as he was sucked into the funnel of grain. He could not hold him and he watched his cousin pulled into the corn where he suffocated.

The incident happened in the early 1990s and I remember the investigation like it was yesterday. I had to interview the surviving cousin. That was one of the hardest conversations I ever had because you could picture every word he described and you could feel the pain he felt for his loss. My memories of the investigation are vivid; but can you imagine how vivid the memory is for the cousin that lived?

Your incident investigations are designed to answer the reason "why" so that you can prevent future incidents.

No one wants to investigate an incident because it reminds you that people are impacted by incidents. But, an investigation process is vital to the success of any HSE program. Investigation processes driven by systematic urgency and discipline prevent future problems when they identify the "real" cause of the problem – AND management takes action to solve the problem(s). We learn from mistakes so that we avoid future interviews like the one I had with the cousin who survived.

Good investigation processes identify root causes and they help identify actions to prevent future failures. A root cause is more than the obvious. The root cause is the upstream source of the injury – a root cause is the one thing that, if taken away, would have prevented the incident in question AND all others similar to it. You will discover that there is usually a series of unwise choices – or "contributory causes" – that lead to the final poor decision that causes the incident. The investigation should also reveal the unwise choices and latent organizational weaknesses – those "contributory causes."

You can use multiple techniques to dig below the surface to discover where the problem started, but one of the easiest is to continue asking "why." Map a series of events that lead to the incident and then document all conditions associated with each event leading to the incident. Then, ask why did each event occur? Why did specific conditions or behaviors occur? Why did people make certain decisions? Why were actions omitted? Ask "why" until you feel you have reached the true and basic source of the problem. Ask until it hurts. You will discover most problems start with a system problem driven by leaders; and if you want to give your organization the opportunity to improve, you have to identify where the system or leadership broke down.

Strong investigation processes also use the value of multiple perspectives. They involve multiple layers of the organization. The employees, the direct supervisor, the manager, and a senior manager should always participate in the investigation process; other "subject-matter experts" or employee representatives should participate as well. If the supervisor and manager fail to participate, they minimize their accountability for the incident and their lack of visibility contributes to a negative safety culture. ACTIVE participation from leadership establishes the level of importance for the incident. But, you also need input from those most at risk – the employees. Dig for the facts with the right people and incorporate the appropriate level of ownership.

What type of incidents should you investigate? You have to investigate any incident that could cause or did cause an injury. You prevent future incidents with exceptional, in-depth investigations. The more investigations you do, the more incidents you prevent.

Do you think the two cousins in the grain silo were the first to experience such a situation? Was that the first time corn had crusted over an auger? Was that the first time they had to use alternative methods to remove grain? Is it reasonable to think that the corn would dislodge at some point? I wonder what would have happened if the leadership had investigated previous near misses – if they had recognized the potential for future incidents through past investigations. I assure you, the situation could have been different if they had!

Minor incidents that occur every day are a precursor to future tragedy. Investigate the small things with relentless consistency so that you don't have to perform those hard interviews like I did with OSHA.

Step 1 (week one)
Where does an organization start in the first week?
   1. *Assemble your RDT to define your strategy.*
   2. *Determine what type of incidents you will investigate.*
   3. *Decide who will be involved with the investigations.*
   4. *Establish who is responsible for leading the investigation.*
   5. *Develop a review process that confirms the team identified the root cause.*
   6. *Develop a reporting protocol.*
   7. *Establish a follow-up process that ensures the appropriate people follow through with corrective actions.*

Critical Implementation Point: *Create an incident investigation process that you know you can follow consistently.*

Step 2 (week two)
How do you communicate the plan in the second week?
1. *Explain the expectations and philosophy for investigations.*
2. *Communicate the value of investigating minor events.*
3. *Train potential team members in root cause identification.*
4. *Promote the importance of reporting all incidents.*
5. *Do not punish people indirectly or directly for reporting incidents.*
6. *Communicate your reporting protocol.*
7. *Incorporate communication opportunities into established meetings.*

Critical Implementation Point: *Training and communication for incident investigations is not a one-time shot. You have to take an ongoing approach to gain the full value of investigating incidents.*

Step 3 (week three)
How do you institute the plan in the third week?
1. *Collect your first incident report.*
2. *Work as a team to investigate the incident.*
3. *Follow your review procedures to evaluate the quality of the investigation.*
4. *Follow through with corrective action procedures.*
5. *Communicate results to all appropriate people.*

Critical Implementation Point: *Incorporate fanatical urgency into your incident investigation process.*

Summary Principle # 3: Worksite Analysis
Organizations have to analyze their processes, identify risk, and investigate events. It is a simple principle with a monumental impact on injury

reduction. A thorough system for worksite analysis also develops safety awareness in the individuals that perform the audits, assessments, and investigations. The characteristics help leaders prevent injuries and they help an organization mature.

I remember when I worked for a previous employer; the corporate organization would schedule corporate safety audits for each facility in a two-year cycle. A corporate auditor would lead a team of auditors. The team included a cross section of site safety professionals from different facilities across the organization. I have one primary impression of the experiences. Even though I knew how to perform audits, I always learned something. Every facility had areas they could improve but they also had successes to share. The successes provided insight that the auditors could carry back to their sites.

As you develop your different methods to analyze work and investigate incidents, remember that the auditor and investigator can also benefit from the experience. Everyone has a chance to learn.

Principle # 4: Hazard Prevention and Control

"Put barriers between the person and the risk."

What stands between you and danger? Risk is inevitable – you have to put barriers between you and the hazard in order to manage the risk. Strong safety cultures understand this principle, and they identify potential risk and they place control methods (barriers) in place.

Do you know where you are vulnerable? Will you do anything about it? Has an unexpected event ever startled you? Yellow jackets are an aggressive bee and they make their nest in the ground. You can disturb their environment when you least expect it. These attack bees were a hidden danger in my yard at a previous home. Every spring I developed a false sense of security because the insects were not active as the seasons changed. Even though I knew the bees were there the year before, I still developed that false sense of security because they were simply not as visible in the spring. Then when I least expected it, they unleashed their assault!

If you have ever been attacked by yellow jackets, you know what I mean. Unknowingly, when I began the summer maintenance on my lawn, I pushed the mower over the yellow jacket nest and the excitement would start - I put on a show for my neighbors as I danced around the yard to escape the reach of dozens of yellow jacket stingers.

Fed up with the cycle, I decided to do battle with the yellow jackets, and I started by putting controls in place. I donned two pairs of warm-ups, two heavy-hooded sweatshirts, a baseball cap, and boots. This was South Carolina, in mid-July; my neighbors thought I was nuts! In full armor and in blistering heat, I intended to seek and destroy the insects, without knowing when they would attack again. I could never find all of the nest. When I destroyed one, another one would appear when I least expected it. Not only did I have to correct the hazard (destroy the nest), I had to prepare for the unknown and wear my gear.

If you can relate to the hidden danger of a yellow jacket's nest, you can relate to hidden dangers in the workplace. Risky conditions and behaviors may remain dormant all around you just like a yellow jacket's nest buried in the ground. When you feel most comfortable with your surroundings, hazards can strike with a vengeance leaving injuries behind.

Don't let your normal routine lull you into a sleepy, false security. Anticipate hidden risks and prepare for the unexpected. Your environment changes and you have to plan for these changes.

In this section, we will focus on three ways you can plan for the routine and nonroutine hazards you will encounter. The goal is to keep at least two defenses between you and any hazard.

Technique #10: Policies and Procedures

Bring clarity and discipline to your culture with fundamental policies and procedures. You can only realize the full benefit of your policies and procedures when you take them off the shelf, dust them off, evaluate them, communicate them, train your staff on them, and enforce them.

Policies and procedures satisfy the requirement for "written programs" in regulations such as confined space entry, lockout tagout, hazard communication, lead work, and respiratory protection. These procedures, these "written programs," provide the requirements that are consistent with those in the regulations that workers must follow in order to be in compliance with the regulations. Still other procedures are written that help protect employees from hazards associated with common activities (not otherwise covered by regulation or industry standard) such as first line breaks, hot tapping, welding/cutting/burning, and heat stress prevention. Managers can't expect employees to know how to behave if there are no written programs and procedures to help them. Procedures help to establish discipline and order in the safety program.

How do all of the policies and procedures fit together to form a cohesive safety program?

Do you like to put puzzles together? I don't mean the wooden puzzles with huge pieces and shapes small children recognize, eat, destroy, or even flush down the toilet. I mean the big 1,000-piece puzzles with complicated colors and shapes that are hard to match. The process can be painful to watch. To put the puzzle together, you start with the corner pieces because they are easy to recognize. Then, collect and connect all the edges of the puzzle. You use trial and error to construct the rest of the puzzle as you put the exact pieces where they belong. There are no duplicate pieces and you see the end of the puzzle when you put the last piece in place. One missing piece will leave you unsatisfied. You start with assorted pieces of colored cardboard and end up with a unique masterpiece complimented by the contribution of every individual piece.

Every regulatory program and site-specific process represents one element—one piece of the puzzle—that has to fit into the overall picture. You start with your cornerstone programs that are easy to recognize and implement such as hazard communication, confined spaces, personal protective equipment, and lockout tagout. These cornerstone programs (that is, corner pieces of your puzzle) build a firm foundation that allows you to complete the edges of your program with processes that define your culture. Once you have identified the pieces of your puzzle – the policies and procedures that will make up your program – you will need to understand the impact of the programs, and communicate roles and responsibilities to your organization. After you develop the policies and procedures, you can begin to train, monitor, and coach employees to help them understand the policies and procedures. Then, you put the policies and procedures into practice (implementation).

Each policy and procedure offers a unique benefit that represents a piece of the puzzle. Your ability to lead with consistency, discipline, and clarity will establish a culture that embraces the policies and procedures that prevent injuries.

Step 1 (week one)
Where does an organization start in the first week?
   1. Assemble your RDT to define your strategy.
   2. Identify all of your policies and procedures.
   3. Determine which ones are your cornerstone procedures.
   4. Evaluate their effectiveness.
   5. Establish consequences for noncompliance with nonnegotiable policies and procedures.

Critical Implementation Point: *Create active policies and procedures that are visible in the workplace.*

Step 2 (week two)
How do you communicate the plan in the second week?
   1. Your goal is to help people understand the purpose and value of the policies and procedures.
   2. Have your RDT go into the field for seven consecutive days and talk with people about the purpose and value of the core policies and procedures. (You may want to put together talking points for each RDT member so that you can communicate a consistent message.)
   3. Promote the value with personal testimonies of how a procedure benefited an employee. Most people can describe a near miss that could have been prevented with the right procedures.

4. Communicate through training: orientations and regulatory training.

5. Communicate through awareness campaigns that include posters, banners, safety talks, newsletters, and alerts.

6. Use all available media to establish the cornerstone pieces of the policies and procedures.

Critical Implementation Point: *Treat your policies and procedures communications as an ongoing process. Focus your communications on the cornerstone policies and procedures first and then fill in the rest of the puzzle.*

Step 3 (week three)

How do you institute the plan in week three?

1. Continue your informal communications and interviews in the field.

2. Monitor compliance in the field.

3. Coach people who do not understand.

4. Reassemble the RDT to discuss what you learned.

5. Make appropriate adjustments.

Critical Implementation Point: *Find a way to make policies and procedures real to people. Share what you have seen and heard.*

Technique #11: Site Rules

Foul ball! Safe! You're out of there! When an umpire waves his arms and yells those words, fans see the impact of the rules with good and bad calls. Every call prompts an emotional response and the application of the rule is visible. Good umpires are knowledgeable, observant, and consistent. They make hard calls regardless of public opinion.

One baseball season, my son Jacob hit a beautiful line drive into right center field beyond the reach of the outfielders. The score of the game was tight and every run counted. With the fans cheering, Jacob rounded all the bases and headed for home. The dugout erupted as Jacob passed home plate, with what appeared to be an "in-the-park" home run. Jacob's team swarmed him after he ran back to the dugout. Then, the catcher from the other team casually walked up to Jacob and touched him with the ball. The umpire screamed, "You're OUT!" The stands erupted again with a different emotion; contempt! According to the umpire, Jacob did not touch home plate! It was a stand up, uncontested, in-the-park, home run – no question about it. But Jacob missed the plate, and the rules said he was out! How was that fair?

The rules decide what is fair. No matter how bad it hurts, you have to play by the rules. Jacob learned a lesson that he will never forget. You have to tag all of the bases if you want your run to count.

Safety rules are similar. Good leaders are knowledgeable, observant, and consistent in the application of rules. Good leaders make hard calls regardless of public opinion. Focus on the simple rules teaches employees to tag all of their bases if they want to work safe.

Compliance with the rules instills discipline into program implementation, and it demonstrates your commitment to safety. Rules have to have clarity. You cannot implement rules with ambiguity and expect success. Establish simple rules with clear consequences. As a leader, make the hard calls and live with the outcome. If you do not clarify and enforce the rules with consistency, you create apathy with your employees. When you enforce the rules – AND administer the consequences – you set the expectations for the future. Employees recognize the limits and they learn from your decisive choices. Rules provide a way to measure individual commitment. In time, your safety culture will improve simply because "the rules" will become second nature; and all will "know" that ignoring a rule just isn't done in your shop! Or if it is, there WILL be consequences!

As one measure of your safety culture, how would you rate your company's commitment to safety? Every organization should establish feasible site-specific rules to which employees must comply. Train employees on the rules and verify they understand. Strong safety cultures have employees who know the rules, and employees have a disciplined approach to compliance with the rules. There is little confusion about right and wrong. The expectations are clear, and the consequences are appropriate and just.

Step 1 (week one)
Where does an organization start in the week?
1. *Assemble your RDT to define your strategy.*
2. *Define your nonnegotiable rules.*
3. *Plan to make the rules visible with a "brand."*
4. *Define the consequences for noncompliance.*
5. *Prepare your team to deliver the strategy with steadfast commitment.*

Critical Implementation Point: Create rules and consequences that your team can enforce.

Step 2 (week two)
How do you communicate the plan in the second week?
1. *Your goal is to help people understand the purpose and value of the rules.*
2. *Have your RDT go into the field for seven consecutive days and talk with people about the purpose and value of the core rules. (Put together talking points for each RDT member so that you can communicate a consistent message.)*
3. *Promote the value of the rules with personal testimonies of how a rule has benefited employees.*
4. *Communicate through training: safety meetings, orientations, and regulatory training.*
5. *Communicate through awareness campaigns that include posters, banners, safety talks, newsletters, and alerts.*
6. *Use all available media to communicate the rules.*

Critical Implementation Point: Communicating the rules is an ongoing process.

Step 3 (week three)

How do you institute the plan in week three?

1. Continue your informal communications and interviews in the field.

2. Monitor compliance in the field.

3. Coach people who do not understand.

4. Keep a scorecard on compliance with the rules.

5. Reassemble the RDT to discuss what you learned.

6. Make appropriate adjustments.

Critical Implementation Point: *After you have trained, communicated, and coached people on the purpose and value of the rules, administer the consequences with relentless persistence.*

Technique #12: Pretask Planning

"I just wasn't thinking!" You hate to hear comments like this after an incident. An effective pretask plan requires people to think before they act: effective pretask planning will have considered the risks and identified appropriate actions to mitigate identified hazards; an effective pretask plan will minimize risk! This section will ask you to develop tools that encourage crews to evaluate every step of their day so they can consider the risk and the proper way to mitigate the hazards.

Where are the signs! Have you ever desperately uttered these words? I found myself repeating them over and over one day as I tried to get to the airport in New York City. I am accustomed to the small town traffic of my home town in South Carolina. Navigating downtown New York City was intimidating – so before I embarked on my journey, I diligently studied a map. I memorized the most direct route to the airport. My trip into the city progressed as planned until I exited the Holland Tunnel into Manhattan. I found myself on a traffic circle I had failed to identify on the map. As I proceeded around the circle with a 1000 cars blowing their horns at me, I did not see a familiar street. I was confused.

Between the traffic circle, aggressive drivers, and basic confusion, I lost my sense of direction. The experience felt like I was playing the "dizzy bat" game – you know, the one where you put your head on the end of a bat and run around it 20 times. After the 20th time, you stop running in circles and try to race to the finish line without running in the wrong direction. I came out of the traffic circle as though I had been playing dizzy bat - disoriented and going in the wrong direction. I saw plenty of directional signs, but the problem was I had no idea where each sign would lead me. After 45 minutes of touring downtown Manhattan, I recognized a landmark symbol that I had studied on the map before my trip. I followed that series of symbols as though my life depended on each sign. I finally stumbled onto a road leading to the airport. The traffic was heavy, but at least I knew where I was going.

How do you perform a job safely when you are facing the unexpected? Pinpointing the details of a work procedure is like studying a roadmap. You have to look at every step along the way. But you also have to expect to encounter "traffic circles." Surprises prompt the "deer in the headlights" look, so you have to search for surprises, and be prepared for them.

How do you deal with confusion without getting hurt? Number one – don't panic. There is always a way to avoid injury if you keep a level head. As I anxiously toured New York City, I relied on the information I had studied before my trip. I remembered the general location of several streets and landmarks. They did not immediately appear as I exited the traffic circle, but my preparation gave me a general sense of where I needed to go. Safety is similar. You won't automatically have all of the safety answers, but preparation will help minimize the confusion, and lead you in a more orderly fashion. Discipline yourself to learn the controllable elements of your job, and realize there are times when the answers to your questions are not directly in front of you. Progress forward with caution, and look for the safe landmarks and signs that can get you closer to your destination. Confusion will make you anxious - just like wandering through the jungle of New York City; but preparation will help you identify landmarks in your work that will help you generate the right decisions.

There are two critical ways to discipline your organization to preplan work and anticipate risk. These "tools" are Job Safety Analysis (JSA) and Task Safety Assignment (TSA). Each tool addresses different stages of a plan but both tools require you to anticipate, identify, and mitigate risks.

Job Safety Analysis

A JSA evaluates a job – a series of tasks – in its entirety. You can evaluate each step in a job and identify the hazards associated with each step. Once you know the hazards, you can put defenses in place to protect people. A JSA allows you to think through the job as a whole and prepare for individual steps. You perform a JSA before you begin a project. It is similar to a work procedure that identifies risks throughout the procedure. Leaders should use a team approach to develop the JSA. The more input you get from different perspectives, the more effective the JSA tool is.

Task Safety Analysis

A TSA focuses on the risk associated with a specific task for that day. Identify all potential hazards in the work environment. Use the TSA to remind your team of the required permits, PPE, training qualifications, and other miscellaneous safety precautions associated with a specific task for the day. A supervisor should perform a TSA with their crew every morning before employees start work. The crew should use this time as a prejob brief for the day. Have each employee sign the TSA at the start of the shift. Following completion of the task, or at the end of the day, conduct a posttask briefing. The supervisor should document all concerns or incidents that happened that day. Have each employee initial the TSA during the post-shift TSA brief, indicating their agreement with all items on the TSA.

Good pretask planning tools require you to think through all stages of work. Document the process and monitor your system daily so that employees never have to say, "I just wasn't thinking."

Step 1 (week one)

Where does an organization start in the first week?

1. *Assemble your RDT to define your strategy.*

2. *Identify two tools you can use to preplan overall jobs, and individual tasks. Examples: JSA and TSA.*

3. *Develop forms to document the process.*

4. *Decide how you will implement the forms.*

5. *Determine who is responsible for the application and how you will monitor the process.*

Critical Implementation Point: To experience success, you have to integrate preplanning tools into daily task.

Step 2 (week two)

How do you communicate the plan in the second week?

1. *Your goal is to encourage people to anticipate risk before every move.*

2. *Have your RDT go into the field for seven consecutive days and talk with people about the importance of anticipating risk. (Put together talking points for each RDT member so that you can communicate a consistent message.)*

3. *Train people on how to use your prejob planning tool and your pretask planning tool.*

4. *Communicate through training: safety meetings, orientations, and regulatory training.*

5. *Utilize a team approach to develop JSAs.*

6. *Require supervisor to use a TSA every day.*

7. *Communicate through awareness campaigns that include posters, banners, safety talks, newsletters, and alerts.*

8. *Use all available media to communicate your efforts to anticipate risk.*

Critical Implementation Point: Preplanning success requires you to think through to full scope of a job with a JSA and success demands preparation on a task level with a TSA.

Step 3 (week three)
How do you institute the plan in week three?

1. Continue your informal communications and interviews in the field.

2. Monitor the quality of the JSAs and TSAs in the field.

3. Coach people through the different processes.

4. Reassemble the RDT to discuss what you learned.

5. Make appropriate adjustments.

Critical Implementation Point*: Continue to improve your preplanning tools with a scorecard.*

Summary Principle # 4: Hazard Prevention and Control

Your goal is to prevent hazards and control the risk. Procedures, policies, rules, and plans help you accomplish this goal.

Preventing hazards and controlling risk is like a drive in the fog? One morning I found myself navigating the fog as I enjoyed my ride to work. I could not see anything around me, so I used extra caution, slowed down, and took my time. I even considered not taking my usual shortcut through the country, because I was unsure what I might encounter in the fog.

Then I had a strange revelation. I thought about how it's odd that you can always see just far enough ahead of you to proceed without problems. Limited visibility slows you down, but you still get to your destination because you take the time to focus on what is directly in your path. You adjust to your environment. You put controls in place such as a safe speed and a heightened awareness to keep you safe.

Driving on a clear day is different. You see stop signs, red lights, crossroads, and cars in the distance and you can prepare for them with advanced notice. You are not restricted by limited visibility, and you can make decisions easier. Your obstacles and detours are in plain site.

Safety is very similar to traveling in the fog. There are times when you have to proceed with extreme caution due to complex circumstances, and like traveling on a clear day, there are times when you have ample warning to react to your changing environment. With both circumstances, you can still reach your destination if you approach the situation with the proper planning and controls in place.

Principle # 5 - Safety and Health Training

"Share what you have seen and heard."

Create a climate where people want to learn about safety and health. You can establish formal and informal methods to create this environment. An effective safety and health training plan has three layers: classroom training, coaching in the field, and general awareness communication. To achieve success at all three levels, organizations have to equip managers with knowledge. Value-added education goes beyond teaching individuals specific skills. Meaningful training teaches people to think about what could happen. Leaders have to dedicate time to development, and they should have support systems in place to follow-up with positive (and negative) reinforcement. A strategic training plan will help develop a culture that includes proactive safety messages.

We Give What We Get

I'm guilty of giving gifts I want to receive. And I've noticed that Christmas is a great time to observe the types of presents people really enjoy. It is also a good way to learn about the "gift giver." I believe you learn more about what people like by observing what they give other people. For example, I have always bought my boys sports-related toys. They have not always asked for these toys, but Christmas is not complete unless my boys get some type of bat or ball. I enjoy sharing these gifts with Caleb, Jacob, and Luke with the hope they will enjoy them as much as I once enjoyed similar gifts. Most parents can relate to this syndrome. I also observed this inclination with my wife Lisa's family. Lisa has two stepbrothers who fly airplanes, and their interest in planes has carried over to their children and cousins. Lisa's stepbrothers extend their passion for planes to the children by giving toys that fly. Their kids have learned to love any type of toy related to aviation. Our gifts help condition our kids to enjoy what we enjoy.

How does safety relate to this picture? We give gifts we value and we teach people the principles we want to enhance for ourselves. If we value safety, we share information that reflects safety values. Organizations must have a passion for sharing the safe habits that someone shared with them. We condition new employees with the safety mindset we teach.

Ask yourself, "Do you communicate and model the safety behaviors that mean the most to you?" Remember, what you give is what you get.

Technique #13: Safety Leadership Training

Safety success rises and falls on the leadership of the organization – and leadership is all about influence. Your learning environment has to teach your leaders how to persuade others to work safe. Leaders have to know how to motivate people to work injury-free. Leaders have to balance positive motivation and consequences for noncompliance to drive exceptional performance. Build your culture with safety leadership training that teaches leaders their roles and responsibilities, tools for safety communication expectations, and techniques they can use to accomplish your HIGH expectations. You also need to equip leaders with the appropriate level of technical safety skills so they can identify and control risk.

The "know how" for safety leadership is vital, but also remember that adults want to know what is in it for them. It is rare that an individual plans to get hurt or they feel like injuries are just part of the job. Combat this lackadaisical attitude by giving people a cause to champion. A "cause" is an objective, a reason, or a motive for working in a common direction. An injury-free environment alone is a good motive to work safely, but a day with no injuries is assumed. An injury-free day does not feel like a reward, and a normal day can create apathy towards safety processes. Avoid complacency and give employees targets, milestones, and achievements to accomplish. Leaders build positive momentum with a "cause" that recognizes achievement.

The cause is more than the day-to-day processes with mundane rewards. The cause is the bigger enticement. The cause is the image of excellence. The cause is the fruit of your labor and the results of your sacrifice. Think about Olympic athletes for a moment. They train relentlessly. Is their ultimate reward the fact that they are great physical condition? Athletes train for much more! They train so they can compete with other skilled athletes and prove they are the best. The "cause" is the opportunity to stand on the stage with the spotlight on the gold medals around your neck. There is value in the process, but there is motivation in the outcome.

Show your leaders "what's in it for them" so that they have a cause to champion. For example, OSHA's VPP program is a tremendous cause to champion and every step towards that cause strengthens your safety culture. The VPP program requires you to implement proven principles that achieve success. The reward is the opportunity to fly the VPP flag at your site. When you achieve VPP, you are a part of an elite group of companies. You benefit from a safer work environment, but you also take pride in the recognition from OSHA. When you achieve VPP, it is like standing on the stage with the spotlight on your medals.

Train leaders on the skills and techniques they need to drive success, but also include a "cause" to motivate your leaders. The cause could be their impact on building the safety culture. The cause can include the milestones you want to achieve. The cause can include a need to address a crisis at your site. There is no magic formula, but keep the motivation in front of people throughout the training – make it even more visible when the training is complete. Frequently reinforce your leaders with the message about why safety is important to them (what's in it for them!) Focus your leaders on their responsibility to protect people – but do not assume that your leaders know how to sway people in the right direction. You may also need to provide training on how to sway people.

Organizations committed to safety demonstrate the depth of their safety culture with the time they dedicate to safety leadership development. Your team will know you mean business when you allocate time to develop their ability to influence safety performance.

SAFETY LEADERSHIP TRAINING TOPICS	
Leadership Topics (This is the WHY)	**Tools and Techniques (This is the HOW)**
1. Organizational Values	1. Demonstrate Your Visible Support
2. Zero Incidents is Achievable	2. Plan for Safety
3. Why Safety is Important	3. Measure Your Accountability
4. The Benefits of a Zero Incident Culture	4. Involve People in the Process
5. The Power of a Leaders Question	5. Analyze Work with Audits
6. How You Will Measure Success	6. Preplan Work with JSAs and TSA
7. Expectations and Responsibilities	7. Train Employees with Safety Meetings
8. Character Traits of a Strong Leader	8. Communicate Your Safety Message
9. How to Motivate People	9. Show Commitment to the Rules
10. How to Communicate Your Message	10. Mentor New Employees

Throughout my career, I have documented leadership qualities I like and dislike. I have compiled a list based on the successes and failures I have witnessed in other leaders. My list knows no organizational boundaries because I believe leadership is a 360-degree concept. A job title does not dictate one's ability to influence. I want to share the list for two reasons: 1) the list identifies qualities that help leaders; 2) the list provides traits that you can choose to develop in yourself and in your organization.

70

QUALITIES I ADMIRE IN A LEADER

1. Serve.
2. Inspire you to believe.
3. Have passion for their cause.
4. Follow-up on initiatives.
5. Communicate a vision.
6. Influence in 360 degrees.
7. Connect with people.
8. Refuse to dwell on destructive issues.
9. Are dependable.
10. Make you want to do better.
11. Can focus people on a "concept" or an "idea."
12. Help you rise to the next level.
13. Do more than what is asked of them.
14. Demonstrate control when frustrated.
15. Are diplomatic.
16. Ask the right questions to make you think.
17. Demonstrate wisdom.
18. Are consistent with a message.
19. Can see the root of the issue.
20. Can be compassionate and firm.
21. Take innovative chances.
22. Recognize the facts and remain positive.
23. Can lead more than a formula.
24. Demonstrate courage.
25. Have specific "nonnegotiable" principles.
26. Do more than dream. They realize the dream.
27. Live above mistakes.
28. Reveal their values with their questions.
29. Help you go places you could not have gone.
30. Can lead despite criticism.
31. Plan and anticipate.
32. Attract people without pursuing them.
33. Draw loyalty.
34. Support their team.
35. Do not take themselves too seriously.
36. Match their actions with words.
37. Refuse dishonest reward.
38. Value honesty.
39. Are firm – they know who they are.
40. Are guided by an idea.
41. Build greater success incrementally.
42. Bring value to those they serve.

You can't expect everyone to embody the full list of admired qualities, but you can decide which traits are most important and relative to the tools we have discussed thus far in the book.

Leadership is more than a policy, process, or procedure. Leadership includes qualities "between-the-lines" that drive the policy, process, or procedure. Make sure you weave the qualities of leadership into the tools you embrace. Here is a sample safety leadership training agenda with potential topics. The goal is to communicate your injury-free vision and provide leaders with the tools to accomplish the mission.

The most realistic perspective you can have is this – your safety performance will never out run your leadership. Set the pace to achieve excellence in performance commensurate with your commitment to develop leaders.

Step 1 (week one)
Where does an organization start in the first week?
 1. *Assemble your RDT and define your strategy.*
 2. *Identify topics you want to present in your training.*
 3. *Coordinate the resources to develop and deliver the training.*
 4. *Allocate the time and money to make it happen.*

Critical Implementation Point: *Leadership development is an ongoing process. Do not approach leadership development as a one-time shot.*

Step 2 (week two)
How do you communicate the plan in the second week?
 1. *Schedule and deliver the training.*
 2. *Communicate the value of continuing the training process.*
 3. *Provide materials that people can take with them.*
 4. *Promote and brand the training so that it becomes a right of passage for leaders.*

Critical Implementation Point: Successful organizations make development a cornerstone to success, and your senior leadership has to make themselves HIGH-LY visible in the process.

Step 3 (week three)
How do you institute the third week?

1. *Complete your training for all applicable employees.*
2. *Give them a task they need to complete once they leave the training.*
3. *Have your RDT conduct informal interviews with participants to confirm and reinforce lessons learned.*
4. *Plan for follow-up training in the future.*

Critical Implementation Point: Safety Leadership Training has to become a staple in your culture.

Technique #14: Dedicated Coach Program

You learn what you see and hear from your coworkers and you modify your behavior based on encouragement from the people around you. A dedicated coach program requires employees to coach each other to do the right things. It is a "my brother's keeper" program.

Training is a vital part of a safety program, but you need some experts in the field to follow-up on the training with practical hands-on knowledge and encouragement. You give employees their initial exposure to the rules and expectations in a classroom, but employees learn how to do their jobs from the people they work with each day. Harness the power of this social dynamic. A transfer of peer-to-peer knowledge carries weight. Take advantage of what happens naturally and designate trusted safety coaches to reinforce training with employees. The program is similar to a mentoring program but the focus is on coaching employees who have been on site for a while. The program also helps show people how to help each other.

Good coaches possess patience and persistence. In the hands of a five-year old, a leaf blower is a disruptive tool. I discovered this when my son Jacob begged to help me blow leaves off our yard one fall day. Thrilled with his willingness to help, I equipped him with safety glasses and earmuffs, and then I explained how to blow leaves. "Line up all the leaves, point the blower in the direction you want the leaves to travel, and blow them toward the desired destination." I even demonstrated a systematic way to sweep back and forth so that the leaves would move together in the proper direction. Jacob was ready!

Jacob started the blower and began to blow leaves with a vengeance. The problem was he blew them EVERYWHERE! After all of my careful instructions, my plans became secondary to the thrill of blowing leaves like a tornado. Over the noise of the blower, I encouraged and coached Jacob. But, Jacob could not harness the power of the blower. When we finally turned off the blower, the leaves were scattered everywhere. Even though I was frustrated, Jacob was content because he had the opportunity to blow the leaves and, of course, to work with dad! Jacob enjoyed his educational experience; and in his mind, the object of the game was to blow leaves at random, where they landed was not important to him. Of course, I had a different agenda, but what an education the experience was for me!

A five-year old is physically and mentally able to use a leaf blower, but the lack of experience and focus was an obstacle to success. Mentoring new employees to work safe is similar. Most employees are capable of performing their job safely but sometimes the lack of motivation, experience, or focus hinders their success and it puts them at risk. The absence of these three elements can become a dangerous variable in the work environment.

How do you protect new employees when you're faced with this risk? Be a good coach. Don't assume that employees have the same culture, the same will, the same "agenda" as you do because it is likely that they do not! Equip employees with all of the safety resources they need, explain the details of the job, AND explain your expectations in both of these areas. Thoroughly explain the risks – and the value of identifying the risks – before they begin a task. Make sure they understand your safety expecta-

tions. Take the new employee step-by-step through the work task if necessary. Reinforce their learning with your encouragement and monitor their
progress. Demonstrate a systematic way to perform the job safely, and
explain the purpose of each action.

With your full attention, employees will give the kind of effort you
expect. Employees will also realize they have to "get a feel for the job"
and may have the tendency to blow the "leaves everywhere!" Your instructions may seem secondary to the thrill of doing the job the way they want
to do it. When faced with the challenge of these moments, a good mentor
will slow the process and continue to coach the employee in the right direction. With a good coach, an employee will harness the power to work
safe through repetition, encouragement, and a thorough knowledge of their
personal responsibilities. Each session is an opportunity to mold and make
more safety leaders and mentors in your workplace.

There are three things that will make a coaching program successful:
1) coaches have to communicate with detail; 2) coaches have to have patience; and 3) coaches have to monitor progress.

The key is to create a structured process that employees value.

Step 1 (week one)
Where does an organization start in the first week?
1. *Assemble your RDT and define your strategy.*
2. *Develop the training material for coaches.*
3. *Identify key points that you want coaches to transfer.*

Critical Implementation Point: Choose coaches with great attitudes.

Step 2 (week two)
How do you communicate the plan in the second week?
1. *Informally interview employees and ask what they wish they had
    learned in the first 30 days they were hired.*
2. *Incorporate what you learn into the training for coaches.*

3.   *Schedule and deliver the training.*

4.   *Communicate the value of coaching in the workforce.*

5.   *Develop a communication campaign that makes coaches visible.*

6.   *Give the training status by the way you talk about it.*

Critical Implementation Point: *Remind people how valuable a long-term coach is.*

Step 3 (week three)
How do you institute the plan in the third week?

1.   *Complete your training for all coaches.*

2.   *Use coaches to reinforce any type of training.*

3.   *Meet weekly with coaches to see how employees progress.*

4.   *Have your RDT conduct informal interviews with participants to confirm and reinforce lessons learned.*

5.   *Plan for follow-up training in the future.*

Critical Implementation Point: *Keep your coaches engaged in the process by communicating with them on a consistent basis.*

Technique #15: General Awareness and Communication

Is it true people have to hear something seven times before they remember it? Research tells us this is true, so apply the concept to your safety communication strategy. To build consistency in your safety culture, surround people with your safety message. Help develop safe habits with memorable and methodical communications.

Sports fans know how to communicate their interest. The universe revolves around football in my house. My enthusiasm towards football began when I was young. My earliest memories include going to Friday night high school football games and watching football on television all weekend. It is a tradition that continues today. Our house is consumed with a message that football is vital to our existence.

I adopted my enthusiasm from multiple influences. I have personal experiences with football. My Dad, brother, and I played football in college. My Dad also coached high school football. There is also a fan side to the story. We watch football on television. There is an anticipation side of the equation; I look forward to football and count the days until it begins. There is an awareness element; we talk about football constantly. There is a visible side to our obsession; we wear our team's colors and purchase "stuff" with our team's logo. There is an educational side too; we read articles and books about football teams and players. And there is a financial commitment to our message; games, tickets, equipment, and promotional material all cost money.

If you did not know my family, how long would it take to determine we like football? NOT LONG! We communicate our enthusiasm for the sport with our words, our actions, our time, and our money. It is not a strategic communication campaign but rather a natural product of our interest. The influence carries over to my three boys. They all play football. I wonder where they acquired their interest. Was it random chance? No, of course not – sports fans *communicate* their interest in the sport. Apply the same principle to your safety culture. If safety is vital to your existence, you have to communicate it with every possible avenue. Your enthusiasm, confidence, and sincerity will become evident to everyone. Your goal is to instill dedication and commitment into your program with a sustained effort to pump your message into your work environment. Let your planets revolve around safety.

Effective communication will come from seven different directions. That could mean seven different people, seven different communication mediums, or seven different training sessions. The idea is to present the message with repetition, enthusiasm, and confidence. Show your passion for safety and sustain the message. Keep it simple but methodical. Also realize that communication is more than an email stating a few goals. Your attitude, confidence, and enthusiasm will communicate what is important to you.

Communication Methods:

Visual: Become safety's biggest fan and make it obvious. Employees should see your injury-free culture everywhere with banners, posters, flags, flyers, letterhead, giveaways, hats, shirts, jackets, bulletin boards, and any other conceivable method to make safety visible. Brand your message with symbols and logos. Keep the message consistent but change the format frequently.

Verbal: Employees should hear the message from multiple directions. Every member of your leadership team should talk about your message in their sleep. Your workforce will begin to expect the first words out of your mouth are always safety-related. Integrate the spoken word into your environment. Conduct safety perception surveys. Your RDT can complete informal interviews in the field. Require a safety topic before ALL meetings. Develop the ability to ask good safety-related questions. Create an environment that discusses safety informally.

Written Messages: Communicate with newsletters, memos, letters to employees, brochures, and flyers. There are endless ways to put your message into the hands of employees. Keep your message simple and focused like a laser on your core messages. Every written document you produce should have a reference to safety – or, at a minimum, it should incorporate your logo or symbol. Communicate your expectations, goals, and responsibilities. Have people sign documents conveying their commitment. Use technology to put the written word out there. Examples: Web sites, email, blogs, Twitter, Facebook....you name it, you can do it. I even know of one site that posts their safety and health newsletter on the inside of the toilet stall doors! Their newsletter is aptly titled, "The Porcelain Press."

Informal Communication: Your conversations count. Safety is not relegated to a formal safety meeting. People know what is important to you by the content of your questions and conversations. Talk about safety when you eat. Talk about safety when you meet. Talk about safety at the coffee pot. Talk about safety on breaks. Talk about safety outside of work. Talk about safety with your family. Relive accomplishments. The idea is to make safety a topic of every conversation just like a sports fan talks about his favorite team.

Safety communication is like cable television – you have to have the "Headline News" version of your message as well as the one-hour documentary version. Both approaches appeal to different people at different times. Cable stations report on the same events, but each network has its own style. Your average viewer cruises the channels sampling different perspectives on the same current events. Take the same approach with your communications and awareness campaigns. Deliver the same core messages using multiple networks.

Step 1 (week one)
Where does an organization start in the first week?

1. *Assemble your RDT and define your strategy.*
2. *Form a safety communications/awareness team (SCA Team).*
3. *Identify potential areas of communication: verbal, visible, and written.*
4. *Develop your core communication messages.*
5. *Incorporate the messages into your strategy with a long-term perspective.*

Critical Implementation Point: Treat safety communications like cable television; same message…different deliveries.

Step 2 (week two)
How do you communicate the plan in the second week?

1. *Train your SCA Team and enable them to execute the strategy.*
2. *Assign specific responsibilities to team members.*
3. *Start the communication process with a safety perception survey.*

4. *The SCA Team can conduct the survey.*

5. *Order visual communications (banners, posters, etc.).*

Critical Implementation Point: *Your communication/awareness strategy should include appropriate daily, weekly, monthly, quarterly, and annual communications.*

Step 3 (week three)
How do you institute the plan in the third week?

1. *Have your SCA Team begin posting information.*

2. *Conduct informal interviews in the workforce.*

3. *Meet weekly to discuss progress and challenges.*

4. *Execute your strategy.*

Critical Implementation Point: *Adopt a sustainable safety communications strategy.*

Summary Principle # 5: Safety and Health Training

Who learns more – the teacher or the student? I remember one of the first training classes that I had to present to a group of supervisors and mangers at a previous employer. The purpose of the class was to explain a new safety team structure we adopted at our plant. I did not have experience speaking in public and I was nervous. To compensate for anxiety, I spent hours in preparation. I did not want to make any mistakes and I learned every detail of the material we presented. I wanted to anticipate the questions supervisors would have so that I could have the right answers.

I was the teacher but I learned more than the students because I prepared. Think about what your organization will look like when leaders take on a role where they know they have to teach people how to work safe. Expect your leaders to teach. That will help develop a learning culture where everyone benefits. Leadership training, follow-up through coaching, and constant communication offer the vehicles to promote learning culture.

Overview:

What separates the good from the great in safety? Companies that excel in safety and health performance share a common characteristic - they are performance-minded and character driven. Their safety character is defined by fundamental safety values executed with focused techniques. Their performance reflects the depth of their commitment to safety. Progressive safety leaders emulate the five strategic principles in the OSHA's VPP. These principles form the framework for injury-free cultures.

1. Management Commitment
2. Employee Involvement
3. Worksite Analysis
4. Hazard Prevention and Control
5. Safety and Health Training

On a conceptual level, the injury-prevention principles are self-explanatory and logical. But in practice, how do employers translate the concept into meaningful performance? Urgency and discipline with injury-prevention techniques help character-driven companies bridge the gap between safety philosophy and execution.

Principle #1 – Management Commitment

Management commitment is the first step to building a performance-minded, character-driven safety culture. Disciplined commitment enables an organization to make difficult choices that impact safety performance. To take the first step, Top Management (in fact all leaders!) must understand that commitment does not exist unless it is visible and consistent. Actions are a reflection of what people believe about achieving zero injuries. Organizations can institute techniques that enable visibility and commitment.

> **Technique #1: Preproject Planning**
> **Technique #2: Measured Accountability**
> **Technique #3: Strategic Visibility**

Principle #2 – Employee Involvement

Are employees just a number? People want to work for employers that see them as individuals and not just a statistic. Employees want to spend their 8 hours-a-day with coworkers who care. Safety metrics are always important, but to build a safety way of life, ask this, "How do I visibly put people first? Am I building mutual respect?" When the focus shifts from a number to a person, safety initiatives take on a more personal focus. Going personal encourages people to take ownership of safety. Sincere ownership and involvement promotes safety success – in implementation, in compliance, in performance.

> **Technique #4: Safety Champion**
> **Technique #5: Employee Mentoring**
> **Technique #6: Safety Perception Surveys**

Principle #3 – Worksite Analysis

Analysis and measurement drives improvement. Companies can't blindly achieve positive results with safety. Evaluate multiple levels of the program on a continuous basis to ensure adequate protection for employees. Thorough analysis tools allow teams to focus attention on areas that count. The main goal is to create a strategic analysis plan that identifies and addresses risk before an injury occurs. Measurement of implementation and compliance will help focus resources and attention in areas in need, as well as highlight those areas where recognition is warranted.

Technique #7: Field Audits
Technique #8: Annual Self-Assessments
Technique #9: Incident Investigations

Principle #4 – Hazard Prevention and Control

There are almost limitless ways to prevent hazards and control risk. The key is to identify the greatest potential for risk and then put feasible controls in place. A hierarchy of controls allows a project to establish a systematic method for minimizing risk. The hierarchy of controls starts with elimination, extends to substitution and engineering controls, following to administrative controls, and finally allows for personal protective equipment when all other controls are either infeasible or "in-the-works." Strong safety cultures use standard systems for controlling risk.

Technique #10: Policies and Procedures
Technique #11: Site Rules
Technique #12: Pretask Planning

Principle #5 – Safety and Health Training

An effective safety and health training plan has three layers: classroom training, coaching in the field, and general awareness communication. To achieve success in all three levels, organizations must equip leaders with the knowledge and the purpose of executing a meaningful training strategy. Value-added education goes beyond teaching individuals specific skills to perform a job. Meaningful training teaches people to think about what could happen. Leaders must dedicate time to training, and they should have support systems to follow-up with positive reinforcement. A strategic training plan will include a variety of consistent and interesting safety messages.

Technique #13: Leadership Training
Technique #14: Peer-to-Peer Coaching
Technique #15: General Awareness and Communication

Conclusion

There is nothing new under the sun. There is no silver bullet to achieve safety excellence. However, there are fundamental principles and processes that WILL MAKE A DIFFERENCE! No doubt readers have implemented many of the ideas discussed here. How do you use the ideas to develop a performance-minded, character-driven culture? You add focus, urgency, and discipline to the process. The proper intentions and motivation will help an organization mature towards an injury-free culture. Commitment, involvement, analysis, prevention, and training are fundamental principles and the injury-prevention techniques translate principles into action. The actions define the safety character in your program and the consistency of actions defines the level of your safety culture.

Attachment One
Critical Implementation Points

Principle #1: Management Commitment

Technique #1: Project Planning

1. Critical Implementation Point: The RDT is successful when they build a safety plan to address a potential crisis.
2. Critical Implementation Point: Success means you never stop communicating the safety and health plan.
3. Critical Implementation Point: Nothing will happen until you convince those in positions of leadership of the value of your safety roadmap, your game plan, and your execution strategy.

Technique #2: Measured Accountability

1. Critical Implementation Point: In sports, coaches lose their jobs if they do not win. Your organization has to treat leadership performance in the same way, because winning with safety means that people do not get hurt.
2. Critical Implementation Point: Your accountability scorecard will succeed if you gain buy-in from your leadership team.
3. Critical Implementation Point: Leaders will not take the scorecard serious until they understand how you score their performance.
4. Critical Implementation Point: Establish the authority of your scorecard with clear consequences for substandard performance and rewards for excellence.

Technique #3: Strategic Visibility

1. Critical Implementation Point: There must be consequences for a lack of participation and visibility in this technique. Without rewards and consequences, the program will fail.
2. Critical Implementation Point: Leaders want practical reasons for why their visible activities add value. Reinforce the message and communicate the purpose.
3. Critical Implementation Point: Establish the expectation for strategic visibility, communicate the value, monitor progress, and follow through relentlessly.

Principle # 2 - Employee Involvement

Technique #4: Safety Champion

1. Critical Implementation Point: Do not put anyone on the safety champion team that has a remotely negative attitude. They will poison the group.
2. Critical Implementation Point: It will take time for employees to build trust in the Safety Champion Program. People respond to positive results. Plan your strategy to communicate successes in the Safety Champion Program.
3. Critical Implementation Point: It will take time for your safety champion team to settle into their roles. Remain patient and work through the transition by giving your team a cause to work towards.

Technique #5: Employee Mentoring

1. Critical Implementation Point: Don't put anyone in a mentoring position that has a remotely negative attitude. They will poison the group.
2. Critical Implementation Point: Plan your strategy to commu-

nicate successes in the Safety Mentoring Program. You have to highlight the difference people make.

3. Critical Implementation Point: To succeed, the Safety Mentoring Program cannot loose site of the primary purpose of the program. You have to empower peer-to-peer learning through a formal process, and leaders have to constantly nurture the program.

Technique #6: Safety Perception Surveys

1. Critical Implementation Point: The success of the Safety Perception Survey process is contingent on the team's ability to ask the right questions and respond appropriately to the trends.

2. Critical Implementation Point: Make the Safety Perception Survey process transparent. To get legitimate data, people will have to feel the process generates a positive response.

3. Critical Implementation Point: For the Safety Perception Survey to succeed, you have to distribute the survey to a wide audience, identify the trends, acknowledge the drivers, and address the weak portions aggressively.

Principle # 3: Worksite Analysis

Technique #7: Safety Perception Surveys

1. Critical Implementation Point: Keep your audit program simple; consistency in your audit program is more important than complexity.

2. Critical Implementation Point: Over-communicate the standards you will audit.

3. Critical Implementation Point: The ultimate audit program eliminates repeat findings. Give the audit program teeth with rewards and consequences.

Technique #8: Self-Assessments

1. Critical Implementation Point: Know your management system and assess the effectiveness with a team.
2. Critical Implementation Point: Over-communicate the standards you will assess and use a team approach to your annual assessment.
3. Critical Implementation Point: The ultimate audit and assessment program eliminates repeat findings and it is a teaching tool.

Technique #9: Incident Investigations

1. Critical Implementation Point: Create an incident investigation process that you know you can follow consistently.
2. Critical Implementation Point: Training and communication for incident investigations is not a one-time shot. You have to take an ongoing approach to gain the full value of investigating incidents.
3. Critical Implementation Point: Incorporate fanatical urgency into your incident investigation process.

Principle # 4: Hazard Prevention and Control

Technique #10: Policies and Procedures

1. Critical Implementation Point: Create active policies and procedures that are visible in the workplace.
2. Critical Implementation Point: Treat your policies and procedures communications as an ongoing process. Focus your communications on the cornerstone policies and procedures first and then fill in the rest of the puzzle.
3. Critical Implementation Point: Find a way to make policies and procedures real to people. Share what you have seen and heard.

Technique #11: Site Rules

1. Critical Implementation Point: Create rules and consequences that your team can enforce.
2. Critical Implementation Point: Communicating the rules is an ongoing process.
3. Critical Implementation Point: After you have trained, communicated, and coached people on the purpose and value of the rules, administer the consequences with relentless persistence.

Technique #12: Pretask Planning

1. Critical Implementation Point: To experience success, you have to integrate preplanning tools into daily task.
2. Critical Implementation Point: Preplanning success requires you to think through to full scope of a job with a JSA and success demands preparation on a task level with a TSA.
3. Critical Implementation Point: Continue to improve your preplanning tools with a scorecard.

Principle # 5 - Safety and Health Training

Technique #13: Safety Leadership Training

1. Critical Implementation Point: Leadership development is an ongoing process. Do not approach leadership development as a one-time shot.
2. Critical Implementation Point: Successful organizations make development a cornerstone to success, and your senior leadership has to make themselves HIGHLY visible in the process.
3. Critical Implementation Point: Safety Leadership Training has to become a staple in your culture.

Technique #14: Dedicated Coach Program

1. Critical Implementation Point: Choose coaches with great attitudes.
2. Critical Implementation Point: Remind people how valuable a long-term coach is.
3. Critical Implementation Point: Keep your coaches engaged in the process by communicating with them on a consistent basis.

Technique #15: General Awareness and Communication

1. Critical Implementation Point: Treat safety communications like cable television; same message…different deliveries.
2. Critical Implementation Point: Your communication/awareness strategy should include appropriate daily, weekly, monthly, quarterly, and annual communications.
3. Critical Implementation Point: Adopt a sustainable safety communications strategy.

About the Author

DAVID G. LYNN, CSP, is a Corporate Health, Safety, and Environmental Manager at the Fluor Corporation based in Greenville, South Carolina. Fluor is one of the world's largest construction and engineering firms and they are known for their ability to execute complex projects with exceptional health & safety performance. Fluor has been recognized by Occupational Hazards Magazine as one of America's Safest Companies, and OSHA has also accepted Fluor into their Corporate Voluntary Protection Program (VPP).

David began his safety career in 1992 working for OSHA as a Compliance Officer. He conducted safety inspections that included audit, complaint and fatality investigations. David witnessed how the good and the bad managed health and safety across a variety of industries. The regulatory perspective helps David see his job with a well rounded point of view.

David's regulatory background enabled him to transition into an Environmental, Health, and Safety Engineer's role at a battery plant in South Carolina. The facility manufactured AA & AAA batteries for North America. For 5 years, David led injury prevention strategies with a large workforce in a high demand industry with unique hazards.

In 2000, David accepted the challenge to work for another fortune 500 company as an Environmental, Health, and Safety Manager during the construction phase of a state of the art manufacturing facility in South Carolina. David managed construction health and safety and he coordinated environmental permitting processes for the site. David was also instrumental in the start-up phases of the plant and he remained as the Environmental, Health, and Safety Manager for the plant until 2004.

David started work with Fluor in 2004 as a U.S. Regional Health, Safety, and Environmental (HSE) Manager based in Greenville, South Carolina. In 2008, David became the Senior Programs Manager for the Corporate HSE group. In this role, David leads a team responsible for corporate HSE training, auditing, workers compensation, substance abuse, regulatory compliance, HSE communications, and high impact corporate programs such as OSHA's Voluntary Protection Program (VPP). In 2008 with the support of Fluor executive leaders, David led the corporate initiative to achieve Corporate VPP status with OSHA.

David is a native of Greenville, SC and he graduated from Furman University in 1991. He has published articles in *Occupational Hazards Magazine, ISHN, PTQ,* and *The Leader.* David also coauthored the book *22 Ways that Will Make You a Champion for Safety and Daily Directions.* He participates as a guest speaker for a different industry associations and conferences and enjoys sharing his experiences with groups that want to achieve success with safety.

Other Resources

Also visit www.david-lynn.com for more information